What people are saying about
Balanced Budget, Balanced Life

"Rollie has done it again. He has skillfully blended his own expertise on this subject, added some relevant Scriptures, and shared real-life experiences to create another best seller: *Balanced Budget, Balanced Life: Ten Steps to Transforming Your Finances.* I highly recommend this book for anyone who wants to take control of their finances."

—Doug Clay
general superintendent, The General Council of the Assemblies of God; author of *Ordered Steps* and *Dreaming in 3D*

"The days of feeling overwhelmed about finances are over! *Balanced Budget, Balanced Life* is full of Scripture, inspiration, and the practical tools you need to manage God's money and to live on mission."

—Michael Martin
executive vice president, Evangelical Council for Financial Accountability; coauthor of *Minister's Tax & Financial Guide* and *Church & Nonprofit Tax & Financial Guide*

"In *Balanced Budget, Balanced Life*, Rollie Dimos provides a practical guide for individuals, couples, and even congregations to handle their finances with solid principles that can provide personal stability and freedom from undue financial pressures. He lays out a clear path for believers to deal with their finances with integrity that results in a strong Christian testimony. The practical worksheets and reflection questions are an added feature of this valuable resource. I personally recommend this book for those needing help to manage their finances and for leaders who have the opportunity to teach these ten principles, especially to young adults."

—Efraim Espinoza
former (retired) director of Hispanic Relations for The General Council of the Assemblies of God; assistant district superintendent, Midwest Latin American District

"*Balanced Budget, Balanced Life* is an excellent resource for anyone looking to improve their financial lives. Rollie's years of experience and practical tips blended with Scripture create a pathway to financial freedom."

—Kyle Dana
senior vice preside t Solutions, al Solutions

D1411326

"With a servant's heart, Rollie has given us ten easy-to-follow steps to help reduce stress and worry over our finances. He keeps it simple: spend less than you earn, create margin, and do it over a long period of time. Thanks, Rollie!"

—Mark Perry
vice president of finance/CFO, Global University

"A married couple once said to me, 'Pastor, money used to tell us what to do, but with the Lord's help we've turned it around. Now we're telling money what to do.' In his book *Balanced Budget, Balanced Life*, my friend Rollie Dimos charts the way to that kind of freedom. You'll find this journey instructive, inspirational, and engaging—truly a gift to everyone seeking financial freedom."

—Dr. James Bradford
lead pastor, Central Assembly of God, Springfield, MO;
author of *Lead So Others Can Follow* and
Preaching: Maybe It Is Rocket Science

"This book will help you see money, stewardship, and your financial future in a whole new light! The message of *Balanced Budget, Balanced Life* is something every person needs to hear from someone who's passionate about seeing people experience liberation from the tyranny of financial frustration. Highly recommended!"

—David Lindell
Campus Ministries director and West Campus pastor
James River Church, Springfield, MO

"Are you ready to experience financial freedom? *Balanced Budget, Balanced Life* will lead you down the path of paying off your debt, living generously, and preparing for your future. While in his previous book, Rollie Dimos greatly assisted churches in handling their finances with integrity, this volume addresses the growing epidemic of inadequate personal financial management that has the potential to threaten your family, hinder your faith, and leave you unprepared for the future. Whether you're drowning in debt or simply desire to sharpen your financial management skills, you'll benefit from this book. The author provides helpful worksheets and practical tips that make it easy to convert your plan into action. The real-life stories will inspire you to stay the course. I recommend this book with enthusiasm to everyone."

—Brad Kesler
network secretary/business administrator, Alaska Ministry Network

BALANCED BUDGET BALANCED LIFE

10 Steps to Transforming Your Finances

Rollie Dimos

Published by Salubris Resources
1445 N. Boonville Ave.
Springfield, Missouri 65802

02-7060

ISBN: 978-1-68067-204-6

Printed in the United States of America

24 23 22 • 3 4 5

For my children, Aaron and Taylor.
You are my inspiration for this book.
May you use these principles to take control
of your finances, change your future,
and achieve financial freedom.

For my wife, Tammy.
Your continual encouragement is the support
I need to overcome obstacles, and your generous
spirit always challenges me to give more.

CONTENTS

Foreword / 9

Introduction / 13

Section 1: Contentment

Step 1: Live within Your Means / 21

Step 2: Use Credit Wisely—Avoid the Obstacle of Credit / 35

Step 3: Reduce Debt / 45

Section 2: Know Your Numbers

Step 4: Set Financial Goals / 61

Step 5: Track Your Spending / 75

Step 6: Create a Spending Plan / 87

Step 7: Stick to the Plan for Long-Term Success / 103

Section 3: Plan for the Future

Step 8: Save for Future Needs / 117

Step 9: Invest in Yourself / 133

Step 10: Bless Others / 149

Epilogue / 161

Appendix A: 102 Ways to Earn More, Spend Less, and Create More Margin / 167

Appendix B: Worksheets / 174

Notes / 185

Acknowledgments / 192

About the Author / 193

FOREWORD

Your first thought might be, *Why do we need another book on financial freedom?* or *What makes this book different than all the others on the same topic?* Those were my initial thoughts . . . until I read it.

Rollie Dimos is a friend of mine. He's a key person on a national team that oversees and manages the finances of a worldwide denomination. So, I knew he was qualified to write on the subject but wasn't sure why he needed to . . . until I read it.

It seems to me that every assignment or task God gives His church comes to us through a chosen leader—a leader who doesn't have the gifts, skills, or resources to accomplish the task on their own. Whether a pastor, missionary, evangelist, or denominational leader, they can only speak about and begin to take steps toward the assignment. Until others bring their talents and finances to the vision, it will never be achieved. The assignments of God require all of us to bring our abilities and resources to the table, which Rollie has done with this book. That's why it stands apart from other books on the subject. He keeps the God-purpose for finances clearly at the forefront.

This book won't ask you to stop fulfilling the God-given purpose for finances or break from the biblical process of tithing while you pursue freedom through a human model. Here the author calls us to adhere to Scripture while applying practical and proven methods to our financial thinking. Rollie starts with the biblical process as a foundation for common sense, well-calculated actions that will produce not only financial freedom but kingdom advancement.

This book isn't written just to set a person or family free from financial struggles, but to help believers be more effective in fulfilling God's assignment for their lives. Like me, the best way for you to know why we need another book on finances is . . . to read it!

—Rick DuBose

general treasurer,

The General Council of the Assemblies of God;

co-author of *The Church That Works*

Rollie and Tammy's Story

It was our first Christmas together. The pressure was on to give a gift that would demonstrate our deep affection for each other. Since one of our first dates was on the ski slopes in Iowa (yes, there are a couple of hills in Iowa), I thought a romantic and meaningful gift for my sweetheart would be her own set of snow skis. While I could probably have afforded new equipment, I settled on purchasing used skis and boots at a local swap meet. Of course, I was elated at giving her such a functional gift with very little expense.

Christmas morning arrived, and my wife-to-be was excited to receive such a thoughtful gift—even though she quickly realized the boots were a size too small. But since the boots were used and couldn't be returned, I reasoned that the only viable option was to remove some of the bulky insulation to make extra room for her feet. To her credit, she was a very good sport to go along with this "no-cost" solution even though without adequate room for her toes or proper insulation from the cold, her feet would always go numb after a few minutes in the snow.

INTRODUCTION

While I can laugh at the story now, this man who thought used, size-too-small ski boots were the perfect gift was me. My wife and I soon figured out that while handling money can be difficult for one person, it can be even more difficult for two people to find the right balance when they view money so differently. When we married, my wife and I did not have the same financial goals. We did not see eye-to-eye on how we should spend money either:

- She wanted to make purchases to decorate the house, I wanted to save money;
- She wanted to buy furniture on monthly installments, I wanted to use cash;
- She wanted to go to the movies, I wanted to rent the movie and watch it at home;
- She wanted to eat out, I wanted leftovers;
- She made frequent trips to the salon, while I cut my own hair;
- She liked to give things away, while I preferred to keep things in storage.

Because God created us with different personalities, it makes sense that we have different likes and dislikes, and different gifts and abilities. For me, the thought of creating a spreadsheet and tracking income and expenses is exciting, while my wife dreads the thought of looking at a column of numbers. I love a good bargain and it takes a little effort for me to part with my money. On the other hand, my wife is more generous with friends and causes dear to her heart. She helps me to be more charitable. Most likely one of us is easier for you to relate to.

Different Personalities, Same Need for a Balanced Life

God created each person with a unique personality. Listen to how the Psalmist described it: "For you created my inmost being; you knit me together in my mother's womb. I praise you because I am fearfully and wonderfully made; your works are wonderful, I know that full well" (Psalm 139:13–14). God created you as a unique human being. The design of who you are, including your personality, isn't a mistake—God has His fingerprints all over you.

Our unique personalities cause us to view money through different lenses. We view the purpose of money in different ways—sometimes in opposing ways. However, we all have the same need for a balanced life, which includes a healthy financial future where we are in control of our money. We need to break free from overwhelming debt, break free from the anxiety and stress caused by late payments and creditors' phone calls, break free from family arguments and hurt feelings, and break free from despair and hopelessness.

I readily admit I'm a numbers guy—I've had a personal budget for many, many, years. I view money as a tool that can help me achieve my goals and bring security to my life. In contrast, my wife, Tammy, is a free spirit with money. She can be happy and satisfied with money, but is also perfectly content without it. For her, money is utilitarian and just one of many tools to navigate life. She would rather know the bottom line than participate in the entire budget-creation journey. She's comfortable in knowing how much we can spend and how much we need to save in order to meet our goals.

Because each person views money through a different lens, a book about managing money will be exciting to some and daunting to others. In each of the ten steps in this book, I'll present the technical details for the subject matter, including charts and templates for you to use to get a balanced budget. But if numbers aren't your favorite pastime, don't worry! I'll also provide practical tips to help you grasp the point of these technical exercises and still achieve success of living a balanced life. There'll be something for everyone—no matter what your personality and view of money.

Saver or Spender?

My friend Steph is a self-proclaimed saver while her husband, Matt, is a spender. Even though they have opposite views on money, they embrace the fact that God created them both, their specific personalities, and their differing thoughts about money. Oftentimes in marriage, one of these personality types will be viewed as the villain, but the truth is both can work together to enrich each other's lives. As Steph describes it, "The saver makes sure there's enough money to live on, and the spender makes sure life is worth living."

Steph makes a good point. The difference between savers and spenders isn't just how they view money, but how they value life. While savers tend to value life in quantity, spenders tend to value life by quality. Savers are motivated by how much they can earn, or how much money is in the bank account, while spenders are motivated by creating experiences or making memories. Together, spenders and savers participate in a balanced picture of how God values life—both in quality and quantity.

Maybe you can relate to the spender or perhaps you relate more closely to the saver. No matter your view of money, this book is designed with you in mind and provides the necessary steps to help you find balance and achieve financial freedom.

The Power and Pitfall of Money

Unfortunately, while money is necessary to navigate life, the process of earning, saving, and managing money is difficult for most people. Managing money is a common stress point in our lives. It's a common cause of tension and arguments in relationships, and an underlying cause of anxiety.[1] Money is the topic that causes the most disagreements for newlyweds.[2] And almost one-third of couples admit to having disagreements about finances at least once a month.[3] As a result, some couples choose to ignore the topic altogether: 12 percent of married people admit they have never talked to their spouse about money, while 26 percent admit they usually avoid talking about finances.[4] When couples do talk about money—or rather, argue about money—they argue most often about merging their money, dealing with debt, budgeting, investing, money secrets, and saving for emergencies.[5]

Even with all the self-help books, television and radio shows, and financial planners available in the United States, recent studies show that too many people struggle with finances. It's highly probable that as you read through the following studies, you'll identify with some of these statistics.

- A Gallup poll found only 32 percent of Americans prepare a household budget each month to track their income and expenses, and only 30 percent have a long-term financial plan that outlines their savings and investment goals.[6] This means almost 70 percent of Americans don't have a budget or long-term financial goals.

- Two similar studies showed that many American families are on the verge of financial disaster. One study reported that 50 percent of American families are living paycheck to paycheck.[7] The other study found that 49 percent of employees report being "concerned, anxious, or fearful about their current financial well-being."[8]

- A survey of minimum-wage workers found that 70 percent say they're in debt, 66 percent struggle to make ends meet, and 50 percent have more than one job in order to make ends meet. Regardless of the salary, 75 percent of employees live paycheck to paycheck to make ends meet at least some of the time.[9]

- Regarding saving for a rainy day or the ability to handle unexpected expenses, half of all Americans have little set aside. Thirty-one percent of Americans have less than $500 saved for emergencies, and 19 percent of these don't have anything saved for an emergency.[10]

- Low income isn't always to blame for financial hardship. About one in five people making $100,000 or more live paycheck to paycheck, and almost one in four people making between $50,000 and $100,000 live paycheck to paycheck.[11]

Let me repeat a few of these statistics: nearly 70 percent of Americans don't use a budget to help manage their money. It's no wonder 75 percent of employees live paycheck to paycheck at least some of the time, and 70 percent say they're in debt.

These statistics are the real-life consequences of not having a budget and sticking to it. The people these statistics represent didn't plan on being in debt or having financial problems, which is exactly the problem: they didn't have a financial plan!

If you identify with any of these statistics, my prayer for you as you read this book is that you'll be motivated to create a financial plan and change the trajectory of your life.

Action Steps

1. If someone watched how you have handled money for the last thirty days, would they say you are more of a saver or a spender? Why?

2. What is a favorite memory or experience you have had that you spent money on?

Section 1

CONTENTMENT: A HEAVENLY PERSPECTIVE ON FINANCES

Step 1
Live within Your Means

"Then he said to them, 'Watch out! Be on your guard against all kinds of greed; life does not consist in an abundance of possessions.'" Luke 12:15

The Bible has a lot to say about money. There are about 2,350 verses related to money,[12] and Jesus spoke on the topic often, incorporating it into sixteen of the thirty-two parables. From the statistics I shared in the introduction, it's obvious that many people, even people of faith, have financial struggles. A committed relationship with God doesn't inoculate us from money troubles.

I won't presume to tell you how to live your life, what to spend your money on, or how much to save, but I will point you to the Book that has the authority to speak into your finances: the Bible provides principles to help us enjoy personal financial freedom.

The Power of Contentment

In 2017, many scholars celebrated the five-hundred-year anniversary of Martin Luther's treatise, which ushered in the Protestant Reformation. Luther challenged the religious culture of the day by supporting the priesthood of all believers and stating that the Bible, not tradition, should be the sole source of spiritual authority. Starting with his ninety-five theses, Martin Luther made great contributions to unlocking the mysteries of the Bible and helping Christians grow and mature in their personal relationship with God. One little known revelation attributed to Martin Luther is this: There are three conversions for a believer—the mind, the heart, and the pocketbook. While this is meant as a joke, I suspect it rings true for many of us.

This reminds me of the story about the man who was being baptized in water one Sunday morning. As the pastor began to submerge him, the man lifted his arm out the water, clutching his wallet to keep it dry. The new believer was ready to commit every part of his life to God except his money!

Having a relationship with God means submitting ourselves to God's purposes and relinquishing control of our lives to His divine purpose. But relinquishing control of our wallet or checkbook doesn't come easy for some. It's a difficult conversion because so many of us think wealth and material goods are the key to happiness. We wonder if we give God control of our finances whether we'll have enough left to make us happy.

Many people aren't happy or content in their current circumstance because they think the grass is greener on the other side of the fence. But this thinking is shortsighted. On a global scale, most Americans are wealthy. While 71 percent of the global population is considered poor or low income, only 5 percent of Americans fall in those categories. On the other hand, only 29 percent of the global population

The Baptism

© 1994 by Thom Tapp. Used with permission.

is categorized as middle-income or higher, but 95 percent of Americans would fit in this category.[13]

By a Global Standard, Majority of Americans Are High Income

% of the U.S. and global populations by income in 2011

	Poor	Low Income	Middle Income	Upper-Middle	High Income
Global	15%	56	13	9	7
U.S.	2%	3	7	32	56

Note: The poor live on $2 or less daily, low income on $2.01–10, middle income on $10.01–20, upper-middle income on $20.01–50, and high income on more than $50; figures expressed in 2011, purchasing power parities in 2011 prices. People are grouped by the daily per capital income or comsumption of their family, the choice of metric depending on how the source for a country are collected.

Source: Pew Research Center analysis of data from the World Bank PavcalNet database (Center for Global Development version available on the Harvard Dataverse Network) and the Luxembourg Income Study database.

PEW RESEARCH CENTER http://www.pewresearch.org/fact-tank/2015/07/09/how-americans-compare-with-the-global-middle-class/ (accessed June 17, 2019).

Based on these statistics, more Americans should have reason to be content with their financial situation. Unfortunately, we're constantly bombarded by advertisers who tell us we need the latest fashion, the newest car, a bigger television, a smarter gadget, and a larger house. How do we counteract the unrelenting clarion call to get more?

Randall Barton summarized it this way: Contentment in our personal finances "is found by having a heavenly perspective on our earthly needs."[14] And finding contentment in your present circumstances is the first step to financial peace.

In the Gospel of Matthew, Jesus talked about accumulating material wealth and the juxtaposition of storing treasures in heaven, rather than on earth. In Matthew 6:21, He summarized this teaching by stating, "For where your treasure is, there your heart will be also."

Contentment is being satisfied with what we have and not looking to material goods to bring happiness.

How we deal with our personal finances indicates what we value or treasure in our lives. It also shines a light on the condition of our hearts and, to a great deal, can demonstrate where we ultimately put our trust—in God or in ourselves.

The Bible has a lot more to say about finding contentment by placing our trust in God. Consider these three verses:

" 'Therefore I tell you, do not worry about your life, what you will eat or drink; or about your body, what

you will wear. Is not life more than food, and the body more than clothes? Look at the birds of the air; they do not sow or reap or store away in barns, and yet your heavenly Father feeds them. Are you not much more valuable than they?'" (Matthew 6:25–26)

"The blessing of the LORD brings wealth, without painful toil for it." (Proverbs 10:22)

"A faithful person will be richly blessed, but one eager to get rich will not go unpunished." (Proverbs 28:20)

In Matthew 6, Jesus reminds us that the first step to contentment is to place our trust in God for our daily needs. Put away worry and anxiety because God our Provider has a heavenly storehouse to meet our every need.

And in Proverbs, chapters 10 and 28, we're reminded that wealth is a blessing from God, given to us without anxiety or trouble. However, these two verses are also a warning against self-sufficiency. If you seek wealth instead of God's provision and direction, you'll be frustrated and in bondage to your lust for more and more, which will ultimately bring you to ruin. You won't have peace until you bring your attitude about money under submission to God's will. Accumulating wealth isn't about satisfying our wants and desires, but about using our resources as God directs us.

Finding Contentment

It's true that a heavenly perspective on our money helps us find contentment, but walking hand in hand with contentment is moderation. Moderation is a key to getting your finances under control.

Entering adulthood, my wife, Tammy, had a crash course on moderation. Her parents divorced while she and her siblings were young. Her mom worked her way through nursing school, which meant that finances were tight for a single parent with three children. The family received government aid, and Tammy helped pay for groceries by babysitting. When she got her first job and a steady income, she wanted to enjoy some of the "luxuries" she couldn't afford growing up. She wanted to eat out, buy nice clothes, and go to the movies. She admits she felt like a kid in a candy store. From a life of lack, she wanted to enjoy all the pleasures of life. Unfortunately, she began to spend more than she earned and ended up with delinquencies, overdraft fees, and an empty wallet. She realized she had to change her view on money and learned how to moderate her behavior in order to get control of her financial situation.

Moderation is defined the same way regardless of your income. No matter your lifestyle, moderation is similar for each of us. It doesn't mean we have to drive a certain type of car or live in a certain type of house or shop at a certain type of store. Instead, moderation means we place limits on our spending habits, so we'll spend less than we earn. Sometimes this is called "creating margin" or "building reserves," and it results in having money left over after all the bills are paid.

Moderation is necessary to create margin. However, moderation for me may not be the same as moderation for you. It does require all of us to evaluate our priorities and ask God how He would have us spend our money—or rather His money.

Listen to this statement by Randall Barton: "Moderation and contentment, stemming from a practical faith in God's provision, are the keys to true happiness and financial success."[15] Read that sentence again and let it sink in. True contentment doesn't come from amassing material wealth; placing our faith and trust in God's provision is the key to achieving financial peace.

God's Money or My Money?

I wonder if much of our financial stress and anxiety is due to a misunderstanding of our money. Is it God's money or my money? Another way of asking the question is, "How much is God's money and how much is mine?"

Many of us see this as a question of percentages and will readily affirm that the tithe belongs to the Lord. But Gary Hoag, the "Generosity Monk," said it best: "We must move from 10 percent thinking to a 100 percent mind-set."[16] This is the same point that Randall Barton makes when he encourages, "We must come to the point where we acknowledge God owns not just 10 percent, but 100 percent! We must let go of being owner and become faithful stewards of what the Master has entrusted to us."[17]

So, as you move along your financial journey, I want to encourage you to seek God's direction before completing each step. Some experts might suggest you stop giving tithes and offerings to your local church until you have your financial house in order. But this is backward thinking! Remember, God owns it all, and we are merely managers of His resources. Keep being obedient with your tithes and generous with your offerings during this process. You've probably heard this before about tithing, but it's worth repeating here: God can do more with your 90 percent than you can do with 100 percent.

Remember, contentment and moderation are the keys to reducing stress and anxiety in your finances. The first step to achieving financial success is to recognize that God is our Provider, the One who created our wealth (Deuteronomy 8:18), and the ultimate owner of all our resources. And God is generous! As you are generous with the resources He has entrusted to you, I know He'll be overjoyed and return His blessing to you "a good measure, pressed down, shaken together and running over" (Luke 6:38).

Tips for Success

As I noted earlier, the statistics are clear: managing finances causes many people a great deal of stress. Look at this financial contentment scale. Where would you place yourself on the scale?

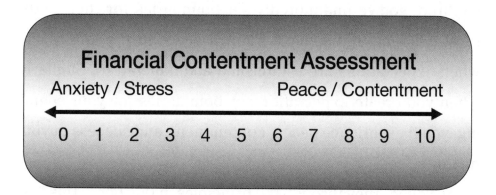

If you're married, would you and your spouse be at the same place on the scale?

A study by Ameriprise Financial found most couples (77 percent) said they were in harmony with each other and on the same page when it comes to managing their household finances. However, this research discovered that even with good communication about money, there are times when couples disagree with their partner's money habits. In fact, about one-third of couples disagree on finances at least once a month.[18] Another study found the most common reasons for these disagreements were about major purchases, decisions about finance and children, or their partner's spending habits.[19]

If you haven't created a plan to control your finances, you have no boundaries or guardrails to your spending. While boundaries may have a negative connotation, these guardrails can bring peace and contentment. For example, if you have children, you've undoubtedly set boundaries for their activities, conduct, and speech. There's peace in the family unit when expectations are established and adhered to. Similarly, when you create expectations or boundaries for your spending, you'll experience peace, contentment, and success in your finances.

As you journey through the principles in this book, this first step to financial freedom can be summarized this way:

- Be content in your current situation.
- Be moderate in your spending.
- Be generous in your giving.

To be content in your current situation doesn't mean you settle for a life of financial stress or bondage, but you realize that peace and happiness aren't achieved by accumulating more stuff. The grass isn't greener on the other side of the fence! Instead, you should change your behavior to spend less than you make to create margin in your finances. As you progress through these steps, continue to be generous with your finances and follow God's leading as you seek financial peace. As you master these three principles, you'll gain greater control of your money rather than your money having control over you.

A word of caution, though. If you're married, or have a family, be careful of using your newfound financial goals as justification for being stingy or controlling your finances too tightly to the detriment of your family. It's important to bring everyone along on this journey. Use the opportunity to teach your family these same principles and give them time to take ownership and adopt these goals as their own.

This will bring great contentment to you and your household, and you'll soon realize you don't need everything you thought you needed before. You may have heard the saying, "He who dies with the most toys wins." Well, that spending motto will put most people in financial bondage, not financial freedom.

Stick with these principles and your goal will no longer be instant gratification or trying to "keep up with the Joneses." Instead, you'll find your tastes will change, and it will become more appealing to save money instead of having the next fad, shiny car, or latest gadget. Financial freedom will be your goal and destiny.

Troy and Angela's Story

I (Angela) was raised in a home where money and finances were a closely guarded secret. My parents never seemed to have money, yet they always had plenty of things (and the debt that went with it). My husband, Troy, was raised in a home where money was a bit like a handout, but was also accompanied by heavy debt.

We married young and without much financial training, so the basis of our financial knowledge centered on credit cards and loans. We walked into marriage in debt and with a negative balance in our checkbook. After a few years we found ourselves drowning in debt, barely making the minimum monthly payments, and clueless about how to manage our finances.

We knew we needed help, so we began a personal finance course. We read and studied the concepts, met with experts, and started saving for an emergency fund. It was both exciting and brutal and, at times, seemed impossible. However, we applied ourselves, ate at home when we wanted to eat out, used a free Redbox code when we wanted to see a new movie, turned off our TV subscriptions, and took advantage of online shows—you get the point. We stayed focused and worked hard, picking up extra work besides our main jobs.

Today, just a few years later, the financial aspect of our lives is forever changed. We paid off approximately $54,000 in debt and are just $4,500 shy of paying off all our debt. Our children are all learning financial concepts at a young age and are making wise decisions with the help of our acquired wisdom and leading. As a family, we are well on our way to full financial freedom. If we can change our financial path, anyone can!

Prayer

Heavenly Father, as I start this journey toward financial health, help me put my whole trust in You for all my daily needs. I realize that I can only achieve contentment and financial peace by placing my trust and faith in You instead of accumulating more and more material things. Amen.

Action Steps

1. Regarding money, how would you answer the question, "How much is God's and how much is mine?"

2. If answering that question is difficult, make it a priority this week to ask God to help you become a faithful steward of all that He has entrusted to you while letting Him be owner of it all.

3. Review the financial contentment assessment scale in this step. Make a list of the things that are causing you stress or keeping you from peace and contentment.

4. What actions can you take this week to help move you along the scale toward peace and contentment?

5. If you're married, discuss your financial contentment assessment score with your spouse. What actions can you take as a couple to move you toward peace and contentment?

Step 2
Use Credit Wisely—
Avoid the Obstacle of Credit

"Keep your lives free from the love of money and be content with what you have, because God has said, 'Never will I leave you; never will I forsake you.' "
Hebrews 13:5

I want to highlight a couple of hazards along the road to financial success. For some, these are merely bumps on the road, but for most people they're concrete barriers that can bring any forward momentum to a complete stop.

The first obstacle to financial freedom is credit. One of the most common ways to lose control of your finances is through excessive use of credit.

The Credit Card Trap

In the 1970s, Americans, on average, saved 9.6 percent of their income.[20] Years ago, many people were accustomed to creating margin in their financial lives and saving money. Unfortunately, this trend has not continued. By 2014, the average American decreased their savings rate to 4.4 percent, except millennials who had a negative savings rate of 2 percent.[21] This means millennials were spending more than they made.[22]

How can you spend more than you make? By using credit cards and delaying your payments until sometime in the future. Unfortunately, if you can't pay off the credit card bill each month, the credit card company will charge you interest, which ends up making it more difficult for some people to pay off the entire bill.

Interest fees on credit card purchases are at their highest point in many years. According to CreditCards.com, interest rates for credit cards are breaking records, ranging from 13 percent to almost 24 percent.[23] Paying interest on credit card purchases is an unnecessary expense and will disappear from your budget if you simply use cash for all purchases.

We must not fall into the trap that the credit card companies have our best interests at heart. Certainly, they won't let us borrow more than we can afford, right? Unfortunately, that isn't the case. Credit card companies will charge you a late fee and interest for unpaid balances, but they won't stop you from charging more! One expert stated that credit card companies will allow people to borrow 250 percent more than they can conceivably repay.[24]

Have you looked at your credit card statement lately? While credit card companies will allow you to pay a minimum balance each month, they also tell you how long it will take to pay off the balance by only making minimum payments. I recently looked at a credit card statement with a balance of $2,300 and the minimum payment was only $27. That's a very convenient payment. However, when I looked closely, the statement made it clear that by making only minimum payments it would take eleven years to pay off the entire balance, and with interest the total amount paid would double to about $4,600. This assumed that no other purchases would be made with the credit card! I think you'll agree that making payments for eleven years, including an extra $2,300 in interest, is not a good use of your time or money.

If you were to talk to my wife, Tammy, she would tell you that a credit card was the primary vehicle to her early financial struggles. When she graduated high school and started her first job as an adult, it didn't take her long to open a store account at a large clothing retailer. On Fridays, she and her cousin would go to the mall and shop for clothes. Tammy would put her purchases on the store credit card. She didn't earn very much, so she could only make the minimum payments each month. However, she continued to shop and buy clothes with her magical credit card, and it didn't take long for her to max out her credit limit. At nineteen, she was already delinquent on her bills and incurring overdraft fees. Without a plan to control her credit card spending, she had to defer her school loans just to stay current with her other bills.

Tammy showed tell-tale signs that her credit card spending was out of control. Consider your own finances. Do they include any of the following signs that your credit card balances are too high and hurting your financial situation?

- You are only making minimum payments.
- Your credit card limits are maxed out.
- You are opening new credit cards to pay off existing balances.
- You are paying bills late.
- Creditors are calling about delinquent payments.

Declined purchases, delinquent bills, and calls from collectors can certainly add a lot of stress to your life. If you have any of these tell-tale signs, consider taking a "fast" from credit cards. Stop using credit cards and concentrate on finding extra funds to pay off your balances.

Tips for Success

Credit cards can quickly jeopardize your success towards financial freedom. Without discipline, it's too easy to let spending get out of control. According to research, people will spend more when they use a credit card than if they used cash.[25] Since credit and debit cards are used more often than cash, there are many opportunities to let your spending get out of control.[26]

If you're not careful, you can quickly end up in a vicious spending cycle that looks like this:[27]

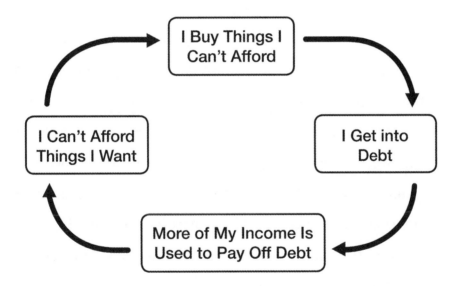

Consequently, I want to encourage you to take a break from credit cards if you're just starting your budgeting journey. Instead of using credit cards, try using the cash envelope system, which I explain in detail in step 7. Limiting yourself to cash, checks, and a debit card can help you get your spending under control.

Paying cash for all purchases will mean that you will have to delay some purchases until you can accumulate the appropriate amount of funds. Make a goal for these large purchases, add it to your budget, and start saving each month. Remember our discussion about moderation in step 1? Not using credit cards for everyday spending will take a combination of moderation and determination to be successful.

It may also be helpful to delete your stored credit card information from online stores and mobile apps. While saving your credit card information for future purchases is a time-saver and makes the online shopping experience more user-friendly, it also makes it easier to purchase an item without giving it much thought. The extra time it takes to find your credit card and enter the information may give you additional time to contemplate the purchase and decide whether it can wait until you have the available cash.

You may wonder if there are appropriate times to use credit cards. I would encourage you to use credit cards only if you can pay off the entire balance each month and avoid late fees and interest. Credit cards may be used when it is more convenient than paying by cash or check, or when carrying cash would not be safe or secure (e.g., traveling). However, in all cases, there should be available funds in your budget to pay off the credit card balance each month. If you are only making minimum payments, you are just saddling yourself with additional debt.

Josh and Laura's Story

My wife, Laura, and I met in college. We were both studying to go into the ministry, deciding that even though ministry isn't the most lucrative business, we wanted to be obedient to what God was calling us to do. Our first position out of seminary was a church plant in St. Louis, Missouri, where we served the church for little and most often for nothing. I ended up getting a job working with homeless people in downtown St. Louis to help pay the bills. However, when we added up my salary from the social service agency and what we got from the church, we were about $5,000 short per year to pay our expenses.

During that time, we continued to tithe faithfully, and I can honestly say God truly provided for us. We served at that church for three years, during which time we never quite made enough money to break even, yet we never missed a rent or utility payment, and we were able to pay off our car! At the end of that season we left St. Louis with less debt than we entered and a few thousand dollars in our pocket!

After St. Louis, we moved to Springfield, Missouri, and things improved financially. During that time, Laura and I felt God was calling us to get out of debt. We had been trying to pay off student loans for most of our marriage and didn't have a ton of success. We had paid off a small amount using the debt snowball method (more about this in step 3), and we often did without and sacrificed to pay off more debt. Progress was slow, and it seemed like we would never get out from under it.

Two years ago, as we were praying about our goals for the year, we felt we needed to pay off our debt by the end of the year. When we did the math, things just didn't add up; there was no way we could afford to do it in a year. If nothing ever went wrong, if our kids didn't outgrow their clothes or have birthdays, we would be able to pay it off in two to four years! However, we both felt that we needed to pay things off that year.

When it was time to make a missions pledge that year, I felt God told me to give a tithe (10 percent) of everything we owed to missions. It was a bit unconventional, but I felt it was what we were supposed to do. So, we saved up and wrote the check to missions. Then we fasted for a week, praying for God's blessings on our lives. A few days later, our son got in an accident and had to spend a night in ICU, thus increasing our debt by a few thousand dollars. This wasn't the response we thought we would get from fasting and prayer. However, we continued to pray in faith that God would go before us.

Within a few months, I got a raise when I switched positions, out of nowhere the church offered Laura a job, and childcare worked out. To top it all off, one of our old insurance companies contacted us and told us they would cover one month of the year for us 100 percent and they randomly picked February and said that was the only month they would cover. It just so happened February was the month our son got hurt. With my raise and Laura's added income, plus insurance covering the medical bills, we were able to pay off our debt by the end of November that same year. God is faithful!

Prayer

Heavenly Father, I don't want my credit card debt to jeopardize my financial freedom. Help me have the discipline to control my spending and be content in my present circumstances. Amen.

Action Steps

1. Make a list of your credit cards and balances. Does this list overwhelm you?

Review the list of tell-tale signs that your credit card balances are too high (page 38). Do you have any of these signs?

2. Consider taking a "fast" from using credit cards. Use only cash to make purchases and don't make any more purchases using credit cards so that you can concentrate on paying off the balances.

3. What other actions can you take to reduce your reliance on credit cards?

4. If you're married, discuss your credit card habits with your spouse. As a couple, what actions will you take to control your spending and reduce credit card debt?

Step 3
Reduce Debt

"Let no debt remain outstanding, except the continuing debt to love one another, for whoever loves others has fulfilled the law." Romans 13:8

In step 2, I mentioned that credit cards are one of two hazards on the road to financial freedom. The second obstacle to financial freedom is debt.

Benjamin Franklin had this to say about borrowing: "He that goes a borrowing goes a sorrowing."[28]

As I mentioned earlier, debt is a widespread problem for many people. From all walks of life, no matter their wage or salary, people are struggling with debt. Consider these statistics:

- Total American household debt has reached a staggering $13.29 trillion. This includes mortgage debt, home equity loans, credit card balances, student loans, and auto loans.

- The average mortgage debt is $181,176.
- The average student loan debt is $46,950.
- The average auto loan debt is $27,669.
- The average credit card debt is $15,482.[29]

The Problem with Debt

Debt slows down, and often blocks, our ability to achieve financial freedom. Making payments to pay down loans makes it feel like we're always looking backward instead of looking forward. The burden of debt can be overwhelming and stressful in our relationships. As stated earlier, about 31 percent of couples disagree on finances at least once a month.[30]

Debt is like a crushing weight on your shoulders—the longer you carry it, the heavier it feels.

In order to put debt into perspective, it's important to understand God's attitude about debt. The Bible doesn't characterize debt as sin, but it does provide warnings about being in debt. Consider what it says in Proverbs 22:7: "The rich rule over the poor, and the borrower is slave to the lender."

Scripture is clear that we need to look to Christ for all our needs, but through debt we allow ourselves to become a slave to the lender. We give the lender authority over us. We put our trust and confidence in a banking institution or credit card provider to meet our needs. Through debt, we are pulled away from

Christ's freedom and provision and tethered to institutions and systems.

From studies and statistics mentioned earlier, we know that debt can increase stress and anxiety in our lives and create conflict in our relationships. Debt also hinders our ability to respond to financial emergencies in our lives.

Debt can also prevent us from responding to God when He prompts us to help others in need.

Consider what your life would look like if you no longer had to make debt payments. For many, that would free up an extra $100, $500, or even $1,000 each month. Not only would you be able to create surplus or margin each month and be better prepared for financial emergencies, you would also be available to respond should God ask you to help others.

If you want to achieve financial success, you need to reduce your current debt and stop incurring more debt.

While I recommend reducing debt as much as possible, and as soon as possible, there can be appropriate uses for debt. For example, many people will find it impossible to buy a house or finance a college education without loans. But it's wise to avoid automobile loans and credit card debt while trying to get control of your finances.

You might ask, "How much debt is too much?" The mortgage-lending industry reviews two metrics before approving loans. One metric is called the debt-to-income ratio or DTI. The industry recommends that your DTI should be less than 35–40 percent. To compute this ratio, divide your total monthly debt payments by your total monthly gross income. A person with a DTI over 35–40 percent may have a difficult time paying all their bills.

The other ratio used by the lending industry is the housing expense ratio. This is computed by dividing total monthly housing expenses by total monthly gross income. If the ratio is more than 28 percent, this also may indicate a potential difficulty to pay all your bills.

These ratios are just guidelines but can be used as a benchmark to measure your own spending habits. (You'll find a worksheet at the end of this chapter to help you get started.)

Debt Snowball Method

So, what should you do if you recognize that you have too much debt?

One way to reduce your current debt is by using the debt snowball method. Many popular financial plans use this tool because it's easy, effective, and helps reduce interest charges by accelerating debt payoff. The goal of this method is to pay off one debt quickly and then apply your newly freed-up cash to help pay off another debt. As you pay off debts one by one, you'll gain momentum like a snowball rolling down a hill.

To reduce your debt using the snowball method:

1. List your debts from the smallest balance to largest balance.
2. Make minimum payments on all debts except the one with the smallest balance—allocate as much money as possible to that one. Once that debt is gone, add these extra funds to pay down the next smallest debt and continue making minimum payments on the rest.[31]
3. Repeat this process as you plow through the remaining debts.

It's not an overly complex process, but it does take determination and willpower to stick with it. Writing it down can be a helpful and motivating tool to keep the end goal in mind. (I've included a worksheet at the end of this step to help you get started.)

Tips for Success

Be careful about "same as cash" offers. These are agreements where you won't incur interest for a certain amount of time, such as six or twelve months, if you make regular payments. In some cases, you may not even need to make payments for the first few months. These can be tempting offers to make purchases even though you don't have the money up front. The "catch" to these arrangements is that if you don't make the final payment by the due date you'll end up incurring all the deferred interest. This extra expense can put a great strain on your finances if you aren't expecting it.

If you can't pay your bills or create margin at the end of each month, it's extremely important to reduce your debt. It may be necessary to take a second job for a while to create additional funds. You may want to sell some items to create additional funding. It may even be helpful to trade in an expensive car for a more economical vehicle. In the most extreme cases, you may want to consider downsizing your home for a more modest dwelling to get out from under the burden of a mortgage. This may seem extreme, but you may decide this sacrifice is necessary for a couple of years in order to have many decades of financial peace and success.

If you believe that your debt is keeping you from achieving financial success, you should make a commitment to get out of debt as quickly as possible. The debt snowball is an effective method to do this, but will require dedication, commitment, and extra funds in your budget to apply to your debt. Any amount applied to your debts will have a significant impact in the long run. Many people who diligently work on their debt snowball will be able to significantly reduce their debt in one to two years. What can you do to find an extra $50, $100, or even $200 each month to start your debt snowball?

The debt snowball has two great benefits. On one hand, it's an effective method to get out from under the burden of debt. On the other hand, once you have freed up money you were using to pay down debt, you can redirect those funds for retirement or other financial goals.

Let me illustrate how effective the debt snowball method is by reviewing two scenarios using the typical American debt of $134,058.[32]

In scenario 1 (page 52), Aaron has three remaining debts: the mortgage on his house and two credit cards. Making the minimum required payments, he's scheduled to pay on these loans for fifteen years or 180 months. Instead, Aaron reviews his expenses and realizes he can make some sacrifices to reduce spending and finds an extra $200 per month to apply to his debt. With these extra payments, he can pay off his three loans in eight and a half years, which is seventy-eight months sooner than originally scheduled, and he has freed up $1,768 per month to reallocate to other financial goals.

If Aaron invests this money at 8 percent for the remaining seventy-eight months he was scheduled to make debt payments, he will end up with an investment totaling about $181,000. Instead of just paying off his debt in 180 months as originally

Scenario 1: Aaron's Debt Snowball

Debt / Creditor	Total Payoff	Interest Rate	Length of Loan in Months	Minimum Payment	Extra Cash + Minimum Payment	Months to Payoff
Home Improvement Store	$1,100	26.99%	70	$44	$44 + $200 = $244	5
MasterCard	$16,748	17.01%	157	$650	$650 + $244 = $894	22
Mortgage	$116,210	4.25%	180	$874	$874 + $894 = $1,768	75
Total	**$134,058**		**180**	**$1,568**	**$1,768**	**102**

Scenario 2: Taylor's Debt Snowball

Debt / Creditor	Total Payoff	Interest Rate	Length of Loan in Months	Minimum Payment	Extra Cash + Minimum Payment	Months to Payoff
Home Improvement Store	$1,100	26.99%	70	$44	$44 + $200 = $244	5
MasterCard	$16,748	17.01%	157	$650	$650 + $244 = $894	22
Furniture Store	$17,200	29.99%	259	$688	$688 + $894 = $1,582	13
Medical Bills	$20,157	0.0%	120	$168	$168 + $1,582 = $1,750	12
Car Loan	$28,948	2.99%	60	$520	$520 + $1,750 = $2,270	13
Student Loan	$49,905	4.45%	120	$516	$516 + $2,270 = $2,786	19
Total	**$134,058**		**259**	**$2,568**	**$2,786**	**84**

scheduled, by focusing on the debt snowball he will have opened the door to achieve some of his financial goals, such as funding his children's college or starting his retirement fund.

In scenario 2, Taylor has six loans that might be typical for a recent college graduate, including the American averages for student loan, car loan, and credit card debt. Making the minimum required payments, she is scheduled to pay on these loans for over twenty-one years (259 months). Instead, Taylor gets a second job on weekends and makes an extra $200 per month to apply to her debt. With these extra payments, she can pay off her six loans in only seven years and has freed up $2,786 per month to reallocate to other financial goals.

If Taylor invests this money at 8 percent for the remaining 175 months that she was scheduled to make debt payments, she will end up with an investment totaling $925,000. Instead of just paying off her debt in 259 months as originally scheduled, Taylor has set herself up to meet her financial goals that include retiring when she wants and on her own terms.

* * * *

You may have a similar situation to one of these scenarios. In both cases, by finding an extra $200 a month, the total debt was eliminated several years earlier than planned. Then by investing the freed-up money that would have been spent on debt repayment, these scenarios created significant nest eggs for retirement or other financial goals.

Gary and Jan's Story

My husband, Gary, and I have had debt all our married life—for thirty-two years. When we married, it was a second marriage for both of us, so we brought debt into the marriage. We both have always had good jobs, so we couldn't understand why we always lived paycheck to paycheck.

We're now approaching retirement age and, for the first time in our lives, are realizing the importance of paying off our debt before we retire. I recently attended a retirement seminar and one of the things they discussed was paying off all debt before you retire, including your mortgage. That was a foreign concept to me, but I left that seminar considering how we could best pay off our debt. I was reminded about the debt snowball method where you pay off your debt smallest to largest, so I went home and made a list of our debt. I have to say it was a bit overwhelming, but we made a commitment to tackle our debt.

When we started this process, we had five or six credit cards with approximately $750 on each of them and another one with about $8,000 on it. I had a couple of personal loans at my credit union (one for $1,000 and one for $5,000), and we had a car loan for $17,000. Our payments for all this debt totaled about $1,800 per month. We never paid the minimums but felt we couldn't afford to pay much more.

With a little determination, we paid off the smaller debts quickly and rolled the payments into the next debt on the list. It felt so good to see the debt going away that I actively started shopping for better prices on cable, Internet, phone, insurance, and security systems. I was able to save about $350 per month just by changing companies or usage plans. Then I started looking at how much I was paying for gas and food. By preplanning lunches and bringing my coffee to work, I saved another $152 a month. I decided to sell my car and find one that would reduce my loan amount. I was able to sell my car for what I owed and bought a less expensive one for around $9,000.

After eight months of using the debt snowball method, we now have about $2,000 that we have freed up to pay down debt each month. We are currently working on the credit union loans, and then we'll tackle the car loan. We expect to be debt free for everything except the house in the next six months—only fourteen months after starting the debt snowball plan. After that, we'll begin paying down our mortgage as fast as we can with the goal to be in a debt-free house by the time we retire. It's a wonderful feeling to know we'll be able to retire without any debt!

Prayer

Heavenly Father, I recognize that I've been pulled away from Christ's freedom and provision through debt. Help me act to reduce debt in my life. Give me peace and success in my finances so that I can respond when You prompt me to help others in need. Amen.

Action Steps

1. Make a list of all your debts. When you look at the list, how does that make you feel?

Does it feel like a heavy weight on your shoulders? Let that feeling motivate you to take immediate action to tackle your debt.

2. Using the Debt Ratio Worksheet, compare your total debt to the benchmarks mentioned.

What immediate changes can you make to get your total debt and housing expenses within these recommended guidelines?

What long-term changes can you make?

3.   Draw up a plan to reduce your debt. Use the Debt Snowball Worksheet to guide you. The success of the snowball method is based on finding extra funds to add to your monthly payment to eliminate your smallest debt. What discretionary spending can be eliminated or reduced to find extra funds?

What are some ways you can create additional income to help pay off debt?

4. If you're married, what actions can you take as a couple to reduce your current debt and keep from incurring additional debt in the future?

Debt Snowball Worksheet

List your debts from smallest to largest.

This is the amount of extra money you can use to pay down debt.

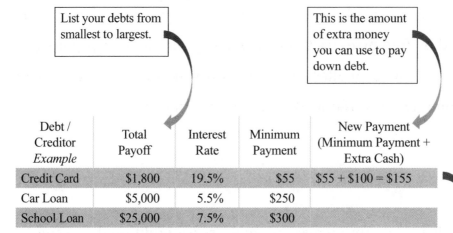

Debt / Creditor *Example*	Total Payoff	Interest Rate	Minimum Payment	New Payment (Minimum Payment + Extra Cash)
Credit Card	$1,800	19.5%	$55	$55 + $100 = $155
Car Loan	$5,000	5.5%	$250	
School Loan	$25,000	7.5%	$300	

Debt / Creditor	Total Payoff	Interest Rate	Minimum Payment	New Payment (Minimum Payment + Extra Cash)
~~Credit Card~~	~~$1,800~~	~~19.5%~~	~~$55~~	~~$155~~
Car Loan	$5,000	5.5%	$250	$250 + $155 = $405
School Loan	$25,000	7.5%	$300	

After the first debt is paid off, use the extra funds to pay off the next debt.

Debt / Creditor	Total Payoff	Interest Rate	Minimum Payment	New Payment (Minimum Payment + Extra Cash)

Debt Ratio Worksheet

Debt to Income Ratio

Total Monthly Debt Payments	$ _____	
Total Monthly Gross Income	÷ $ _____	
	×	100
	_____ percent	

Housing Expense Ratio

Total Monthly Housing Payments	$ _____	
Total Monthly Gross Income	÷ $ _____	
	×	100
	_____ percent	

Debt to Income Ratio (goal is less than 35–40 percent)

To compute this ratio, calculate your total monthly debt payments. Include mortgage or rent payments, credit card minimum payments, auto loan payments, and any other loan payments. Divide your total monthly debt payments by your total monthly gross income. Multiply this result by 100 to get a percentage.

Housing Expense Ratio (goal is less than 28 percent)

To compute this ratio, calculate total monthly housing expenses. Include mortgage or rent payments, interest, real estate taxes, home-owner insurance, and association fees. Divide your total monthly housing expenses by your total monthly gross income. Multiply this result by 100 to get a percentage.

Section 2

KNOW YOUR NUMBERS

Step 4
Set Financial Goals

"Be sure you know the condition of your flocks, give careful attention to your herds." Proverbs 27:23

In the next few steps, we're going to get into the details of creating a budget, but before you create your budget, let's talk about creating some goals for the future.

It's important to create goals to help you move along your financial journey. Maybe you've heard this saying: "You can't manage what you don't measure." If you're not measuring your progress toward financial freedom, you won't know if you're headed in the right direction. Creating goals that are important to you and reviewing those goals on a regular basis will help you determine how you're doing and whether you need to make a course correction.

As you create goals for your financial future, it will be helpful to include short-term and long-term goals. For example, you may want to save $500 for Christmas gifts this year, while contributing 10 percent of your income into a retirement account for the next forty years. Whether setting short-term or long-term goals, it's important to remember two principles about goal setting: make SMART goals and write them down.

Using Goals to Move Forward

The acronym SMART stands for *specific, measurable, achievable, relevant,* and *timely.*[33] A well-designed goal will incorporate these five characteristics:

Specific:	goals should be *specific* and state precisely what you want to do
Measurable:	goals should be *measurable*, with a starting and ending point
Achievable:	goals should be *achievable*, realistic, and attainable
Relevant:	goals should be *relevant*, reasonable, and worthwhile
Timely:	goals should be *time-based*

These are examples of SMART goals you might set for your finances:

- I want to save $500 for Christmas gifts by November of this year.
- I want to increase my net worth by $1,000 in the next twelve months.
- I want to eliminate all my credit card debt in eighteen months.

Remember our discussion about savers and spenders in the introduction? A saver created these SMART goals. The motivation is all about quantity—how much they can save or eliminate in a certain time period. But these goals are missing an important element for the spender—they don't answer the question why we're doing this. They don't focus on quality of life. It can be hard to be motivated by a number if the impact isn't well defined. For example, a goal of "contributing 10 percent from each paycheck into a Roth IRA" may not motivate as well as a goal of "contributing 10 percent from each paycheck into a Roth IRA so that we can retire at age sixty-five and have enough money to travel around the country." Adding the *why* to each of your goals will address the quantity and quality elements that both savers and spenders can embrace.

With this in mind, let's restate those previous examples:

- I want to save $500 for Christmas gifts by November of this year because I don't want the stress of paying off my Christmas credit card debt next February.
- I want to increase my net worth by $1,000 in the next twelve months because I want to be able to quit paying mortgage insurance.
- I want to eliminate all my credit card debt in eighteen months so I can afford to go back to school to finish my degree.

Along with creating SMART goals that include the reason for the goal, it's also important to write your goals down. Our memories can fade over time, but you can review written goals frequently to keep them fresh in your mind. Write them on a notecard and post it on your refrigerator or on your bathroom mirror or next to your computer screen. Let these written reminders motivate you to stick to your plan.

Tammy and I often talk about places we want to visit or new restaurants we want to try or friends we want to have over for dinner. But life happens and our schedules get busy; after a few months, we realize we haven't done any of these activities. When this happens, Tammy will repeat one of her favorite statements,

"If we don't put it on our calendar, it will never happen." Writing your goals down is like putting an appointment on your calendar—it creates a sense of accountability and gives you a better chance at success. You can use the worksheet at the end of this chapter to help you document your goals.

Compute Your Net Worth

One way to measure progress along your financial journey is to review your net worth statement. Your net worth is a picture of your current financial situation. It's an inventory of your assets and liabilities—your cash and investments and your outstanding bills. Your net worth is not static, but is always changing based on your income, spending habits, and investments.

Your net worth is simply the difference between your assets and liabilities—what you own minus what you owe. The value of your house is an asset, but the remaining balance on your mortgage is a liability. Your goal is to increase your net worth over time.

Here are the steps to figuring your net worth:

1. First, list all your assets, including your home, vehicles, bank accounts, investments, retirement accounts, and other valuables like jewelry or coin collections. Then list the value of these assets. You don't have to have an exact

value—a reasonable estimate is good enough. For your house or coin collection, you can estimate the current market value. For bank account and investment accounts, you can list the balances on the most current statement.

2. Next, list your liabilities, like mortgages, car loans, credit card balances, and any other debts you currently owe. Again, if you don't know the current balance, an estimate will work.

3. Finally, subtract what you owe from what you own. The result will be your net worth.

The goal is to have a positive balance that will grow over time as you increase assets and reduce debt. For some, you may be starting off with a negative number, meaning, you owe more than you own. This may happen if you are "upside down" on your car loans, or if you have significant credit card debt or school loans. If you find yourself in this situation, visit some of the tips in steps 2 and 3 to help reduce your liabilities.

If you have a negative net worth, your primary goal is to reduce your debt to achieve a positive net worth. Strive to create margin in your monthly budget by spending less than you make so you can have more funds available to reduce credit card balances, auto loans, and other consumer debt. If you have a positive net worth, your primary goal is to reduce any remaining debt and increase your net assets with savings, investments, and retirement accounts.

Computing your net worth will help you measure your current condition, while creating SMART goals will give you incentive, purpose, and clarity to improve your net worth. (A worksheet is available at the end of this step to help you compute your net worth.)

Tips for Success

Look at your current net worth. Where do you want to be twelve months from now? If you have a negative net worth, what steps can you take to have a positive net worth in twelve months? If you have a positive net worth, what steps can you take to increase it by $1,000, $5,000 or $10,000 in the next year?

What other goals might you set?

- Do you have an emergency fund? A rule of thumb for an emergency fund is to save enough money to cover three to six months of expenses in case you lose your job, get injured for an extended period, or experience a catastrophic property loss. (We'll discuss emergency funds further in step 8.)

- Have you started saving for retirement? If you are forty years away from retirement, a good rule of thumb is to contribute about 9 percent of your income into a retirement account each year. If you have thirty years until retirement, experts suggest you contribute about 17 percent of your income each year.[34]

- Do you have children who want to attend college? Maybe you'll want a goal of putting money aside in a 529 savings account to help with college expenses. A college education is expensive, and the choice to attend either a public or private university will have a considerable impact on the total cost of their education.

Whatever goals you have, computing and reviewing your net worth on a regular basis will help you track your financial condition and assess your progress.

For some people, a long list of goals may seem overwhelming. It may be helpful to just pick one goal to start with instead of trying to tackle all your goals at one time. Look at your list of goals and identify the one that is most important to you right now. In other words, which one of these keeps you awake at night? Tackle that goal first, then you can tackle the other goals one by one as you work through your priorities.

Donavon and Erin's Story

In early spring of 2018, I (Erin) stepped away from a lucrative career to address chronic health issues that had grown increasingly more pronounced. It was a weighty decision, and one that did not come easy. I had spent my entire adult life building a successful career, and had come to find my identity in the excitement of a demanding, full-time job.

My husband is an excellent financial planner and, with the Lord's help, had orchestrated our finances in such a way that we would be able to operate as a one-income family for a short time while I addressed these health concerns. We anticipated a short span of time off, but the weeks transitioned to months and every submitted job application seemed to be met with closed doors.

As the end of summer approached, pressure mounted as our savings account dwindled. My husband and I made my job a key focus of our church's annual focus on prayer and fasting. In the middle of this fast, my husband expressed his concern that our savings account was dangerously close to zero. That same afternoon, I received a call from a potential employer, extending a job offer with the exact salary amount we were praying for. In addition, an attractive benefits package and generous time off was included.

God knows exactly what we need and, in His timing, gives us more than we can ask or imagine. Despite our best and most meticulous budgeting efforts, this season of life proved to us that our ultimate security rests in the One who plans our steps in His divine timing and will. And we learned that our identity can be found not in our careers, but in our calling to be His followers, wherever that journey may take us.

Prayer

Heavenly Father, as I review my finances, please help me to make the changes necessary to improve my financial situation. Help me make worthwhile goals and take the necessary steps to gain financial success. Amen.

Action Steps

1. Use the SMART method to create goals to improve your financial position. Write these goals down using the Financial Goals Worksheet. Consider the following questions to help guide your goals:

    a. Do you need to start saving for retirement?

    b. Do you want to start saving for a college education?

    c. Do you have three to six months of savings in an emergency fund?

    d. Do you have consumer and long-term debt to reduce?

2. Complete the Net Worth Worksheet.

3. Review your goals and your net worth every six to twelve months. If you have a spouse or an accountability partner, be sure to include them in these review sessions. Every time you review your overall financial position, ask yourself these questions:

a. Am I on track to meet my goals?

b. Are there other steps I need to take to get on track to meet my goals?

Net Worth Worksheet

Assets			Market Value
	Cash		
		Cash on Hand	
		Checking and Savings	
		Certificates of Deposit (CD)	
		Cash Value of Life Insurance	
	Investment and Retirement		
		Stocks and Bonds	
		Mutual Funds	
		Pension	
		IRA / 401(k) / 403(b)	
		529 College Savings	
	Property		
		Principal Residence	
		Second Residence	
		Home Furnishings	
		Automobiles	
		Collectibles	
		Jewelry	
	Other		
Total Assets			

Liabilities			Amount Owed
	Unsecured Debt		
		Credit Cards	
		Charge Accounts	
		Student Loans	
		Alimony / Child Support	

Liabilities cont'd			Amount Owed
		Unpaid Taxes	
		Other	
	Secured Debt		
		Home Mortgage	
		Home Equity Loans	
		Auto Loans	
		Boats / RVs / Campers	
		Other	
Total Liabilities			
Net Worth (Assets Minus Liabilities)			

Financial Goals Worksheet

Goal (include the "Why?")	Strategy or Action Steps	When Do I Start?	When Do I End?
Example: I want to save $500 for an emergency fund in the next ten months, so I won't have to use a credit card if my car breaks down.	Save $50 per month.	February 1	November 30

Step 5
Track Your Spending

"Do not wear yourself out to get rich; do not trust your own cleverness. Cast but a glance at riches, and they are gone, for they will surely sprout wings and fly off to the sky like an eagle." Proverbs 23:4–5

In order to make an accurate budget, you must have an accurate accounting of your income and expenses. While you probably have a good estimate of how much you bring home and how much you spend, I find that most people underestimate both categories.

The first step in the balanced budget process is to track your spending activity over time—at least a month and up to six months. This part of the budget creation process isn't difficult, but it will take a little bit of time and research. Before you get started, you'll need to gather your pay stubs or earnings statements, bank statements, check register, credit card statements, copies of past bills, and receipts for cash transactions.

Document Your Income and Expenses

The point of this exercise is to document all your sources of income and determine how much money you spend each month. This is a necessary step before you can create a useful budget.

This important task can take as little as a few hours, but you should refine it over the next few months to ensure you have all your income and spending activity identified. You don't have to wait six months before you create and follow a budget. You can start now, and just update your budget every month if you identify additional income and expense items.

Many times, people will forget about bills that are only paid once or twice a year, instead of monthly. Automobile registration fees may be paid annually while automobile insurance may be paid quarterly or semiannually. To make sure you don't miss these seasonal or occasional payments, look at a year's worth of bank statements or credit card statements to identify these infrequent bills.

When tracking income, include your weekly paycheck, rental income, government assistance, investment income, interest, and dividends payments.

When tracking expenses, be sure to include your regular and irregular (or fixed and variable) spending. Fixed expenses are those payments that occur each week or month, which oftentimes are established by contracts, agreements, or payment schedules and include mortgage, rent, car loans, and some utilities. Irregular or variable spending covers all the other expenses. These expenses may not happen each week, vary with use, and usually involve "treating yourself to something nice" like dining out, entertainment, vacations, gifts, and hobbies.

There are two different worksheets at the end of this step that you can use to track your income and expenses for the next thirty days. Each worksheet includes common expense categories for most households. They also include categories for debt payments, savings, and retirement contributions. You can add more categories if necessary. As you document your transactions, you should accumulate your activity into the different spending categories to help you create a budget in step 6.

After you've documented all income and expenses for a thirty-day period, subtract your expenses from your income. If you have something left over, you have margin or surplus at the end of the month. This surplus can be used to pay down debt or put in savings for an emergency fund. If you have a negative result, you are spending more than you earn. It's imperative to see where you can reduce expenses to create margin. If you can't reduce expenses, you must find additional income to cover your spending. I'll discuss more ways to create margin in steps 6 and 7.

Tips for Success

If you often wonder where your money goes each month, this process of tracking your income and expenses will help you identify your spending habits. If you haven't already done so, create a filing system for key financial and household documents. Whether it's a paper or digital system, it's important to have a central place to keep bills, bank statements, insurance policies, product warranties, credit card agreements, tax returns, and legal documents.[35]

Speaking of digital systems, you aren't limited to the paper worksheets at the end of this step to track your activity. Besides those worksheets, you can use budgeting apps on your phone or computer software. Your banking institution may also offer online programs to help you identify and track all your expenses.

The first time you complete this worksheet, you may find that you don't have enough margin to meet your financial goals in step 4. This is the point where determination and commitment are necessary to achieve your goals. Review your expenses and look for ways to reduce your discretionary spending. Making sacrifices in your spending habits for a few short months can yield great rewards for years to come.

It's not uncommon for people to get a second job when starting their budget journey and/or attacking debt via the debt snowball method. You might have to clean out your closets, have a yard sale, and sell some possessions to increase income. Whatever steps you take to increase income or reduce expenses are important and necessary to change your financial circumstances and gain financial freedom.

Thomas and Noelle's Story

Three years ago, my car was totaled in a minor accident. My parents generously gave us an old Honda Accord with almost 200,000 miles so we could save the insurance payout. We knew we wanted our family to grow and we eventually would need a bigger vehicle. We decided to put the insurance money in a high yield savings account. Over the next couple of years, we added any unexpected money into the "car fund" account.

Last year, we found out we were expecting our third child. Knowing we had some time before we absolutely needed the new vehicle, we started to pray (along with our friends) that God would provide the right vehicle for us. A few months ago, we finally started to look seriously for a van. At the time, we had $8,000 in our car fund and planned on trading in our 2012 VW Passat. We were initially discouraged by the trade-in value for the VW but were committed to our goal of paying cash and not financing the new van with debt.

One Wednesday on our way home from looking at cars at one dealership, I decided to check the inventory at the local Kia dealership. I noticed they had just posted a 2012 Sedona for $10,000. We went straight there to check out the van. It was a basic model but had everything we needed, including a DVD player, and it had only 55,000 miles on it (which was

25,000 less than the VW). The difference between the cash we saved, the trade-in value, and the cost of the new van was only $50. In the end, God provided the right van for us, within our budget, and we even were able to swing an extended warranty.

Prayer

Father God, help me to be diligent about tracking my income and expenses this month. If necessary, help me find ways to reduce my spending or increase my income to create margin in my finances. Amen.

Action Steps

1. Track your income and expenses for one month. Use one of the worksheets at the end of this chapter or a budgeting app on your phone. Your banking institution may even offer an online program that can help. If you are married, complete the worksheet with your spouse to make sure you identify and capture all your income and expense activity.

2. Do you have a net surplus or deficit at the end of the month?

If you have a negative result, what can you do to reduce expenses to create margin?

What additional income can you make to create margin?

Weekly Income and Expense Worksheet

Week Number ____	Income	Taxes	Tithes & Offerings	Housing & Utilities	Food	Transportation	Health & Medical	Personal & Family	Debt & Miscellaneous	Savings & Retirement
						Category				
Sunday										
Monday										
Tuesday										
Wednesday										
Thursday										
Friday										
Saturday										
Subtotals										

Total Income _____

less Total Expenses _____

Net Surplus / Deficit ===========================

Weekly Income and Expense Worksheet

Week Number ____	Income	Taxes	Tithes & Offerings	Housing & Utilities	Food	Transportation	Health & Medical	Personal & Family	Debt & Miscellaneous	Savings & Retirement
					Category					
Sunday										
Monday										
Tuesday										
Wednesday										
Thursday										
Friday										
Saturday										
Subtotals										

Total Income   _____

less Total Expenses   _____

Net Surplus / Deficit   _____

Monthly Income and Expense Worksheet

Day	Income	Taxes	Tithes & Offerings	Housing & Utilities	Food	Transportation	Health & Medical	Personal & Family	Debt & Miscellaneous	Savings & Retirement
1										
2										
3										
4										
5										
6										
7										
8										
9										
10										
11										
12										
13										
14										
15										
16										
17										
18										
19										
20										
Sub-total										

STEP 5: TRACK YOUR SPENDING

Day	Income	Taxes	Tithes & Offerings	Housing & Utilities	Food	Transportation	Health & Medical	Personal & Family	Debt & Miscellaneous	Savings & Retirement
						Category				
21										
22										
23										
24										
25										
26										
27										
28										
29										
30										
31										
Total										

Total Income _____

less Total Expenses _____

Net Surplus / Deficit _____

Step 6
Create a Spending Plan

" 'Suppose one of you wants to build a tower. Won't you first sit down and estimate the cost to see if you have enough money to complete it?' " Luke 14:28

Creating a budget often has a negative connotation. For many, their perception of a budget means restrictions on spending money. It means they can't go shopping or go out with friends or take a vacation.

The truth is, a balanced budget can help you do all of that. If those activities are important to you and part of the goals you identified in step 4, then a budget can help you achieve those goals. Don't think of a budget as limiting your spending—think of it as giving you the freedom to spend on those items that are important to you and are part of your financial plan!

A budget is simply a blueprint or financial plan for what you will do with your income. Sometimes I replace the word "budget" with "spending plan." You need a spending plan to help you take control of your money instead of letting your money control you.

Why Create a Plan?

A budget empowers you to reach your financial goals. There are usually three things we do with income: spend it, save it, or give it away. Once you've identified goals for those three actions, a written plan will help you keep on track to meet those goals. Just like a contractor uses a blueprint to build a house, a budget is merely a blueprint for how you'll allocate your money to certain priorities in your life.

Calling it a spending plan is appropriate because planning is important to God. As we read through Scripture, God gave specific plans to Noah for building the ark. God gave specific plans to Moses for building the tabernacle. God gave specific plans to David for building the temple. And in Luke 14, Jesus referred to the foolishness of the man who built a tower without sitting down first to create a plan and count the costs.

Planning is a worthwhile discipline that yields significant benefits. For example:

1. Planning, like a blueprint, brings clarity to your project and helps you see where you're headed.

2. Planning reduces stress and brings peace to your project. Research shows that 38 percent of married people avoid talking about money.[36] Couples will shy away from this conversation to avoid conflict, but when two people agree to a plan, there will be less chaos and conflict and more openness.

3. Planning helps you prioritize your activities. The goals you set for yourself in step 4 cannot succeed without making those a priority in your spending plan.

4. Planning embraces accountability. With a written plan, you can hold yourself accountable to the expectation. If you're single, invite a friend to hold you accountable to your spending plan. Ask them to pray for you and hold you accountable to your financial goals. If you're married, you and your spouse can hold each other accountable, but confiding in another couple can also be helpful as you navigate the ups and downs of your financial journey.[37]

How to Create a Budget

Let's talk about the specific action points for creating a budget. It's not rocket science, but it does take a little time and effort. Use the worksheet at the end of this step to guide you. To get started, you'll need the worksheet you completed in step 5 that tracked your income and expenses over a thirty-day period.

Action Point 1: Income Compute your net monthly income. This is defined as your total gross income less taxes (federal, state, local, Social Security, and Medicare). Be sure to include all regular forms of income including side jobs, rental income, alimony, and investment income. If you have income that fluctuates each month, you can use the average monthly income over the past twelve months or use the lowest month in the past year as a starting point.

Action Point 2: Expenses Compute your total expenses by spending category. You'll notice that the first expense item on the list is reserved for tithes, offerings, and other charitable giving, which recognizes God's priority in our finances. As I stated in step 5, while it's relatively easy to figure out your monthly expenses, it's easy to overlook bills that are only paid each quarter or once a year. Look at your expenses for the past twelve months to identify these infrequent expenses. These can include auto license and registration fees, insurance premiums, and home owner association fees.

Action Point 3: Savings Add amounts for monthly savings to help you achieve goals for future purchases and expenses like vacations, Christmas gifts, major home and auto repairs, appliances, and furniture. Use your Financial Goals Worksheet from step 4 to help you identify how much you want to save each month to meet these goals.

Action Point 4: Margin Create margin and find ways to increase it. Remember that margin is the term for what is left over after you pay all your expenses. To gain margin, you must spend less than you make. Subtract your expenses from your income to determine if you have margin each month. If you're spending more than you make, you'll have to modify your budget by reducing expenses or increasing income to create margin. When you have margin, you can use this excess to pay down debt, create an emergency fund, increase savings, invest in a retirement fund, save for vacation, save for your child's college education, or bless others by giving it away.

Benchmark Your Spending Plan

If you need to create more margin, you might be thinking, *How much should I spend in each expense category, and how does my spending compare to others?* Look at the following chart. This is what the average American spends in these common categories:[38]

Average Consumer Spending

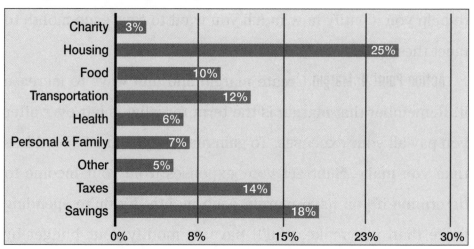

Everyone's financial situation is different, and there's no budget template that will fit everyone's circumstances. However, by comparing your spending plan to others, you can identify spending categories that are significantly different. Under scrutiny, this might yield reductions that could increase additional margin.

Here are two spending plans that might help you assess your own activity.

50/30/20 Plan: One popular spending plan is the 50/30/20 plan. This plan suggests spending 50 percent on "necessities," 30 percent on "wants," and 20 percent on "savings and debt repayment."[39] The "necessities" category (50 percent) includes groceries, housing, utilities, transportation, insurance, child care, and minimum debt payments. The "wants" category (30 percent) includes dining out, gifts, travel, and entertainment. The "savings and debt repayment" category (20 percent) includes saving for an emergency fund, saving for retirement, and paying down debt. This spending model recognizes the importance of savings and that our spending plan normally consists of things that can be classified as either "essential" (necessities) or "nice to have" (wants).

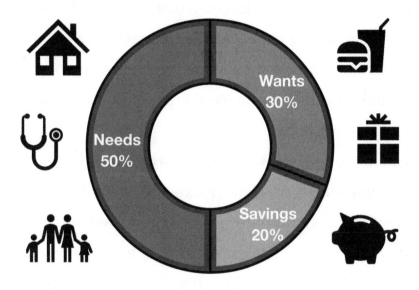

Crown Financial Ministries: Crown Financial offers multiple expense guidelines based on various income levels. These detailed plans list spending recommendations for up to eighteen common expense categories and vary whether you're single, married, and/or have children. An example of their spending guidelines is included at the end of this step. (For more information, you can visit Crown.org.)

Consider using the 50/30/20 plan or one of Crown Financial Ministries' spending guidelines as a benchmark for your budget.

Look for significant differences and see if there are other ways to bring your spending percentages more in line with their suggestions.

Tips for Success

There are two ways to increase margin: either by increasing revenue or reducing expenses. To increase revenue, you can start a second job or sell items online or at a yard sale. Some people find success at starting a side gig like driving for Uber or Lyft or delivering pizzas.

Reducing expenses will take a two-pronged effort. First, look at your budget to identify expense items in the "wants" category. You may find areas for expense reductions in this category and decide that some "nice to have" purchases can be eliminated—at least temporarily. Did you know that if you forego stopping at your favorite coffee shop each morning, you can save about $91 per month?[40] Or, by bringing your lunch to work instead of going out you can save over $1,000 each year?[41]

Unfortunately, many expense items overlap between the "needs" and "wants" categories. For example, business clothes can be an essential need, but a fur coat would be an extravagant expense. You may need an automobile to get to work each day, but a used car might be cheaper and easier on your budget than a shiny, new vehicle.

Reducing expenses in the "wants" category may feel like a major sacrifice, but it's extremely important to find ways to increase margin in your finances. Some of these changes may only be necessary for a short time in order to create the margin you need.

Some of your fixed expenses may be based on contractual agreements, so there may not be a chance for immediate changes. However, you should review your fixed expenses at least annually to see if there are better options for you. In some cases, it may be necessary to sell a vehicle or downsize your home in order to reduce expenses enough to create margin. While these are significant changes, it may be exactly what you need to gain control of your finances. (For more examples and suggestions for creating margin in your spending plan, see step 7.)

Christian and Emilie's Story

Emilie and I have been married for almost one year. We knew from the beginning of our relationship that we wanted to be on the same page when it came to our finances. So, we had many conversations while we were dating about the way we wanted to live and what we wanted to prioritize with our finances.

When we moved to Chicago for my new job, I asked to be paid monthly. We then used a financial planning feature from our online bank to allocate our funds to various areas. Essentially, we created a digital version of the popular "envelope system" of money management. Every month we allocate our funds to rent, utilities, insurance, student loans, groceries, entertainment, etc. This has been a major factor in the way we approach our finances.

Another aspect of the way we approach our finances has been our choice to live off one paycheck. While my wife does work, we pay all our bills and live month to month based off my salary. This requires certain sacrifices, a smaller apartment, and not eating out as often. However, it gives us the ability to take Emilie's paycheck and put it toward debt repayment, our emergency fund, and savings.

Prayer

Heavenly Father, help me create a spending plan that reflects the priorities and goals I've established for my financial freedom. Help my budget demonstrate faithful stewardship of the resources You have provided. Amen.

Action Steps

1. Using your worksheet of income and expense created in step 5, fill out the Monthly Spending Plan Worksheet to create a budget that reflects your financial goals. Do you have enough margin to meet your financial goals?

If not, create a second budget with changes to income and expenses in order to create margin. What steps can you take to put this spending plan into action?

2. Benchmark your spending plan with one of the spending plans described in this step. Are there significant differences? List them here.

What can you do to bring your spending percentages more in line with one of the suggested guidelines?

3. Review your budget every six to twelve months to see if there are ways to further reduce expenses and increase savings.

4.   Once you've created margin in your spending plan, review your financial goals from step 4. Are there additional financial goals you can add to your spending plan, such as:

    a. Saving for an emergency fund

    b. Using the debt snowball method to create more margin by reducing credit card debt, auto loans, and other consumer debt

    c. Saving for retirement

    d. Starting a college savings fund for your children

What other savings goals do you want to add to your budget?

5.   If you're married, review the spending plan together. As a couple, what activities will you prioritize to create margin in your budget and achieve your financial goals?

Monthly Spending Plan Worksheet

	Monthly Totals
Income	
Gross income (paychecks, other income)	$
Less taxes (federal, state, Social Security, and Medicare)	$
Net Monthly Income	$
Expenses	$
Charity — Tithes, offerings, charitable gifts	$
Housing — Mortgage or rent	$
Homeowners and rental insurance	$
Utilities (electric, water, gas, trash)	$
Phone, Internet, cable	$
Real estate taxes	$
Maintenance and repairs	$
Other housing expenses	$
Food — Groceries	$
Dining out	$
Other food expenses	$
Transportation — Gas, parking, and public transportation	$
Car maintenance	$
Car insurance, license, and taxes	$
Car loan payment	$
Other transportation expenses	$
Health — Medicine and prescriptions	$
Medical and dental insurance	$
Life insurance	$
Other health expenses	$

		Monthly Totals
Personal and Family	Clothing	$
	Toiletries and cosmetics	$
	Childcare, school supplies	$
	Child support	$
	Gifts	$
	Entertainment	$
	Pets	$
	Hobbies	$
	Other personal and family expenses	$
Other	Credit card payment	$
	Student loan payment	$
	Miscellaneous	$
Savings	Emergency fund	$
	Retirement	$
	College fund	$
	Extra payments to pay down debt	$
	Other savings goals	$
	Total Monthly Expenses	$

Total Income _____

less Total Expenses _____

Net Surplus / Deficit ══════════════════

Spending Plan Definitions

Income	Gross income (salary, wages, side jobs, dividends, interest, other income)
Charity	Tithes, offerings, charitable gifts
Housing	Mortgage or rent payments, homeowner or rental insurance, utilities (electric, water, gas, trash, phone, Internet, cable or satellite television), real estate taxes, maintenance and repairs, and other housing expenses
Food	Groceries, dining out, and other food expenses
Transportation	Auto loan or lease payments, gasoline, oil, and maintenance, public transportation, parking, tolls, auto insurance, registration, taxes, and other transportation expenses
Health	Medicine and prescriptions, insurance premiums for medical, dental and life, and other health expenses
Personal & Family	Clothing, toiletries, cosmetics, childcare, child support, school supplies and activities, gifts, entertainment, pets, hobbies, and other personal and family expenses
Other	Credit card minimum payments, student loan payments, and other monthly debt payments
Savings	Emergency fund, retirement contributions, college savings fund, extra payments to pay down debt, and other savings goals

Suggested Percentage Guidelines for Family Income

Married with 2 Children

Gross Household Income:	$25,000	$35,000	$45,000	$55,000	$85,000	$125,000
Tithe/Giving	10.0%	10.0%	10.0%	10.0%	10.0%	10.0%
Taxes						
1. Federal*	0.00%	0.00%	1.07%	2.69%	5.88%	8.43%
2. Social Security**	6.20%	6.20%	6.20%	6.20%	6.20%	6.20%
3. Medicare**	1.45%	1.45%	1.45%	1.45%	1.45%	1.45%
4. State*	0.00%	2.00%	2.00%	2.00%	2.00%	2.00%
5. Other*	0.00%	0.00%	0.00%	0.00%	0.00%	0.00%
Total Taxes*	7.65%	9.65%	10.72%	12.34%	15.53%	18.08%
Net Spendable Income:	$20,587	$28,122	$35,676	$42,713	$63,299	$89,900
3. **Housing**	39%	36%	32%	30%	30%	29%
4. **Food**	15%	12%	13%	12%	11%	11%
5. **Transportation**	15%	12%	13%	14%	13%	13%
6. **Insurance**	5%	5%	5%	5%	5%	5%
7. **Debts**	5%	5%	5%	5%	5%	5%
8. **Entertainment / Rec**	3%	5%	4%	7%	7%	8%
9. **Clothing**	4%	5%	6%	6%	7%	7%
10. **Savings**	5%	5%	5%	5%	5%	5%
11. **Health/Wellness**	5%	6%	6%	5%	5%	5%
12. **Miscellaneous**	4%	4%	6%	6%	7%	7%
13. **Investments****	0%	5%	5%	5%	5%	5%

All your net spendable income percentages should add up to 100%

If you have school/childcare expenses, these percentages must be deducted from other categories

14. **School/Childcare*****	8%	6%	5%	5%	5%	5%

*The most accurate way to determine your Federal, State, and Other tax withholdings is to check your last Federal and State tax returns. The numbers on the chart above are only estimates using 2018 tax rates, $4,000 exemption/person, and standard.

**If you are an employee, this is the correct amount witheld from your paychecks. If you are self-employed, the amounts double to 12.4% for Social Security and 2.90% for Medicare.

***In some cases earned income credit (EIC) will apply. It may be possible to increase the number of deductions to lessen the amount of tax paid per month. Review the last tax return for specific information.

****This category is used for long-term investment planning, such as college education or retirement.

*****This category is added as a guide only. If you have this expense, the percentage shown must be deducted from other budget.

CROWN
Do Well
crown.org

(This chart is only for reference. For charts specific to your household, visit Crown.org at https://www.crown.org/resources/spending-budget-guides/)
"Suggested Percentage Guidelines for Family Income," Crown Financial Ministries, https://www.crown.org/wp-content/uploads/2018/08/Married-2-Children.pdf (accessed May 17, 2019).

Step 7
Stick to the Plan
for Long-Term Success

"The plans of the diligent lead surely to abundance, but every one who is hasty comes only to want."
Proverbs 21:5, RSV

For your spending plan to be successful, you must be diligent to follow it. As God promised in Proverbs 21:5, your diligence in following your spending plan will result in abundance—even financial abundance!

God's Word promises abundance for those who follow a plan. You'll certainly see the fruit of your labor as you create margin to start or increase your savings. You'll be prepared to pay for an unexpected car repair. You'll have confidence in your financial future, and you'll have harmony and unity in your family relationships because everyone will be committed to the plan.

I did say you'll see the fruit of your "labor" as you follow your plan. Some of you may think sticking to a spending plan is a lot like labor. It doesn't sound exciting; it feels more like a grueling exercise and hard work.

Remember, your spending plan isn't meant to constrain or restrict you. It's meant to empower you and give you freedom to spend appropriately. As you stick to the plan, you'll reap a harvest of benefits. If you diligently follow your spending plan, you'll significantly shape your financial future. Your plan will:

S: Show you how to get out, and stay out, of debt.

H: Help you develop the all-important habit of saving.

A: Allow you to respond when God prompts you to give.

P: Provide margin for saving, investing, and emergencies.

E: Empower you to live with less stress and more confidence.

Shaping Your Future

Remember the goals you created in step 4? Some of your goals were short-term and some were long-term. Your financial future is like "playing the long game." This refers to constant and active participation in working toward goals that may take a long time to achieve.

Have you ever played chess? To win at chess, you must anticipate your opponent's moves before they happen, and you must plan what you're going to do several moves in advance. Your financial success requires you to play the long game by being actively involved in following, and sticking to, your spending plan.

You may have heard that it takes at least twenty-one days to form a habit. Sticking to your financial plan is like forming a habit. It's probably not something you've done before, and it'll take some time and effort before it becomes second nature to you. You'll need time to change your spending habits, time to change your views about money, time to get out of debt, and time to make headway toward your savings goals. Unfortunately, it's going to take much longer than twenty-one days to be successful. In fact, one study suggests it takes between two and eight months to create a lifestyle change.[42]

Essentially, that is what you're doing—you're changing the way you live. By changing your current behavior, you'll change your future. No longer will you let money control you—you will control your money.

Tips for Success

Even though you're in this for the long haul, there are plenty of short-term actions that will set you up for success. Here are some creative ways to help you achieve some "wins" as you move along your financial journey.

Increase Margin in Your Budget

Here are some ways to increase margin in your budget without much effort—although it will take dedication and intentional action:

- If your family has two incomes, consider living on one and saving the other. Create a spending plan that only includes one income source. You can use the second income source to reduce debt.

- If you are paid on a biweekly basis or twenty-six times per year, consider a spending plan based on twenty-four paychecks, or two payments each month. Use the two extra paychecks to build an emergency fund or save for a vacation.

- Use bonuses and cash gifts received on your birthday or at Christmas to build a retirement fund or start a college savings account.

- Compare your actual expenses to the budget guidelines mentioned in step 6 to benchmark your activity once or twice a year. These guidelines aren't set in stone but can help you spot areas in your spending where you might be able to reduce expenses.

Use the Envelope System to Control Expenses

The envelope system is an easy and effective way to control your spending. It's appropriately called the envelope system because you put cash in different envelopes to help manage your spending according to your budget.

For example, let's assume you have budgeted $300 for food and $150 for entertainment each month. At the beginning of the month, put $300 in an envelope marked "Food" and $150 in an envelope marked "Entertainment." The restriction that you place on yourself is that you can only use money from the appropriate envelope when making a purchase. For example, when shopping at the market for groceries, use cash from the "Food" envelope. When you go to the movies, spend money from the "Entertainment" envelope. When you run out of cash in an envelope, you are done spending in that category until next month.

You can replenish your envelopes on a weekly, biweekly, or monthly basis. Use whichever schedule works for your situation. Using this same example, if you replenish your envelopes on a weekly basis, you would put $75 in the "Food" envelope (accumulating $300 over four weeks), and $37.50 in the "Entertainment" envelope (accumulating $150 over four weeks).

Instead of writing checks or using debit and credit cards, using cash will help you quickly assess your spending habits to get your finances under control. You don't have to wait for the monthly bank or credit card statements to figure out how much you have spent in each category and how much you have left. You'll know just by looking at your envelopes.

You can use envelopes for any category in your budget, although they're especially helpful for categories that fluctuate each month or where you may tend to overspend if you're not careful. Consider using envelopes for the Food and Personal and Family categories to control spending in the areas of groceries, dining out, clothing, and entertainment.

If you run out of money in an envelope before the end of the month, you may be tempted to take cash from another envelope. This is acceptable on occasion, but it may reveal a problem with your spending plan. If you find yourself doing this on a regular basis, consider whether you are committed to your plan. Do you need to change it?

Besides actual envelopes, there are also computer programs and mobile apps to help you manage your spending in a similar fashion.[43] Whether you use cash envelopes or a mobile app on your phone, find a system that works for you.

Avoid Impulse and Convenience Buying

One of the easiest ways to bust your budget is to buy things on impulse. Here are some indicators of impulse buying: you have items around the house that are still in their original packaging, or you have clothes in your closet that still have the price tags on them. Another indication is that you often run out of money in your envelopes before the month is over.

A similar habit is convenience buying. This involves spending money on things that make life easier, but usually cost much more. Dining out or buying take-out food is certainly convenient in our fast-paced society, but it usually costs more than preparing food at home. The latest electronic gadget or device is certainly nice to have, but it usually costs more to be fashionable and trendy.

Here are some ways to avoid impulse and convenience buying:

- Wait three to five days before making a major purchase or buying an item that isn't in your current budget.
- Make sure your spouse agrees with the purchase.
- Look for alternative sources. Shop around and take advantage of discounts, coupons, or price-matching offers.
- Buy seasonal items during the off-season.
- Avoid spending for emotional reasons.
- Don't window shop for entertainment. Find a less tempting hobby!
- Plan your meals and make a grocery list. Only buy what is on your list.

- Cook double batches and freeze meals to reduce dining out for convenience.
- Use "fun money" or "allowance" funds that are included in your spending plan for impulse purchases.

(For additional ideas on how to create margin in your finances, see appendix A: 102 Ways to Earn More, Spend Less, and Create More Margin.)

Reward Yourself

Include a motivational reward in your spending plan for hitting certain goals. Like dangling a carrot on a stick to motivate a mule to move forward, using rewards can help motivate you and your family toward financial goals. For example:

- If you have a goal to save $1,000 in the next twelve months, then set the goal for $1,100. When you hit the goal, take $100 as a reward and spend it on something that isn't in your budget. Treat yourself to a night out or a new outfit.
- If you have a goal to save $10,000 in the next twenty-four months, then set the goal for $11,000. When you hit the goal, take $1,000 as a reward and treat your family to a vacation or purchase some new furniture.

Similarly, if you have extra money at the end of the month in the Dining Out envelope, you can take a portion of that excess as a reward and spend it on something personal like a latte, a massage, or tickets to a ballgame. Rewarding yourself can help boost your motivation and determination, and rewarding your family can keep everyone inspired to work toward the same goal.

Mark and Katie's Story

Mark and I have been married for twelve years. For the first six years of our marriage, I handled our finances. Since I'm the "spender" in the relationship, you can guess how that went. My breaking point was a few days before Valentine's Day when I bought a bunch of gifts for the kids and found out there wasn't enough money left in our bank account to pay our tithes that Sunday. I sat down on our living room floor and cried. I asked God, "How did we get here and how are we going to get out?"

I returned the gifts, which came to the exact amount I needed to pay our tithes. We paid our tithes, and that same week got our tax refund. I told Mark we needed to change the way we handled our finances and suggested he needed to be more involved. He jumped on board with the idea. He's a numbers guy anyway and quickly created a spreadsheet for our budget. He also came up with a system to pay our monthly mortgage out of our tax refund. For six years, we've put our tax money into an account to pay our mortgage and use our full paychecks for other expenses.

It's been great to work together and go through our budget each week to see what we need to change or what we need to focus on. We've never stopped tithing. If we missed a week, we paid double the next time. We've always lived paycheck to paycheck, but God has always provided for our needs. Even when the budget didn't add up, there was always extra. God has made it work and has blessed our finances through raises and promotions. It's amazing to see how working together on our finances has transformed our marriage. We owe it all to God for continuing to provide each week and guide us in our finances.

Prayer

Heavenly Father, my financial journey is going to take time, effort, and patience. Help me stick to my spending plan so I can create margin and enjoy the abundance You promise to those who are diligent. Amen.

Action Steps

1. Use the envelope system for most of the variable categories in your spending plan to help control your spending. Don't use debit or credit cards.

Do you have enough money in the envelopes to get through the month?

If not, do you need to make changes to your spending plan?

2. What changes can you make to reduce impulse buying and convenience buying? (For example, make time each week to prepare and freeze several meals to reduce the pressure for take-out meals.)

3. What rewards can you create to help motivate you to reach your financial goals?

If you're married, or have children, include them in the process so all of you can work toward the same goals. What rewards will help motivate the entire family?

4. Review the list in appendix A. Are there additional ideas you can utilize to increase margin in your monthly spending plan?

PLAN FOR THE FUTURE

Step 8
Save for Future Needs

"Wealth gained hastily will dwindle, but whoever gathers little by little will increase it." Proverbs 13:11, ESV

One of the primary principles in achieving financial freedom is to spend less than you earn. The amount of money that remains after you pay all your bills each month can be set aside and saved for future needs. These needs may be six months down the road or forty years down the road.

You identified these future needs, or long-term financial goals, in step 4. Whether it's saving for retirement, a college education for your children, or a down payment on your first home, you'll need margin in your spending plan (see step 6) and diligence and determination to follow through on your long-term goals (see step 7).

Preparing for a Rainy Day

Many people struggle to save for a rainy day. For example, one in three Americans has less than $500 saved for emergencies, and one in five doesn't have anything saved for an emergency.[44]

This lack of savings is demonstrated by the fact that the personal savings rate of adults has been dwindling over time. In the early 1940s, adults were saving about 24 cents for every dollar of disposable income. It hovered around 10 percent in the late 1970s and early 1980s, but currently, adults are saving less than 4 cents of every dollar of disposable income.[45]

To quote Benjamin Franklin again, "If you would be wealthy, think of saving as well as getting."[46] In order to gain financial freedom, we need to be more diligent about our savings plan. Two savings goals you should include in your financial plan are a short-term and a long-term emergency fund.

Short-Term Emergency Fund

Put aside $500 to $1,000 in a savings account for unexpected expenses that aren't part of your monthly spending plan. When your refrigerator, washing machine, or furnace breaks down, you'll have some funds available to pay the repair bill. Start with $500, and then increase the emergency fund to $1,000 as soon as you can. This emergency fund is meant to give you some peace of mind knowing that you'll have funds available if your car or house needs immediate repairs. These funds are not meant to supplement discretionary spending like clothing, dining out, or going on vacation. When you spend this money on an unexpected expense, you'll need to replenish the savings fund as soon as possible. This may mean reallocating your margin each month and delaying other savings goals.

Long-Term Emergency Fund

Financial experts also recommend an emergency fund to cover the unexpected loss of income if you lose your job or are injured and unable to work. They suggest increasing your emergency fund from $1,000 to an amount that would cover three to six months of your basic living expenses. In case it takes you six months to recover from your injury or find additional work, you'll have funds to sustain you and your family and cover your basic needs.

Whether you need three months or six months will depend on whether your spouse has employment to cover a job loss, or whether you have adequate insurance to pay medical bills or supplement your income if you are injured.

Look at the spending plan you created in step 6. What expenses would you need to cover if you unexpectedly lost your job? What discretionary spending could be reduced or eliminated (like clothing, dining out, and entertainment)? Once you identify your essential expenses, you can multiple this total by three to get a total minimum goal for your emergency fund.

You might wonder if an emergency fund is really that important. Research has proven that having adequate savings is an important factor in providing a feeling of financial security.[47] We know that 50 percent of families are living paycheck to paycheck and up to 75 percent of workers live this way at least some of the time.[48] Tremendous stress results when a person or family is living paycheck to paycheck. But it's not just low-wage earners who feel this stress because these feelings of security are not fully dependent on one's income. Similarly, we know about one in five people making $100,000 or more live paycheck to paycheck.[49]

Having a financial cushion is closely tied to a person's feeling of financial well-being. Without a cushion like an emergency fund people can lose hope.

Saving for College

Many parents have a goal to help fund their child's college education. A qualified tuition program, also called a 529 plan, is a great tool to save funds for your child's college expenses. These savings plans (authorized by Section 529 of the Internal Revenue Code) are designed to encourage saving for college, university, and education costs by providing tax benefits. There are two types of 529 plans: a prepaid tuition plan and an education savings plan. All fifty states sponsor at least one type of 529 plan.

- A prepaid tuition plan lets individuals purchase tuition credits at participating colleges and universities. Purchased at current prices, a beneficiary can use these credits later, which protects the beneficiary from rising education costs. Currently, eighteen states offer prepaid plans, but only eleven are accepting new applicants.[50] A prepaid tuition plan can cover tuition and fees at public and in-state institutions, but doesn't always cover room and board. If the beneficiary wants to use the credit at a private or out-of-state school, the credits may have a lower valuation. These plans are not without risk, though, as some are guaranteed by the state while others are not. You may lose your money if the plan's sponsor has financial trouble. Typically, either the investor or the beneficiary must be a resident of the state that sponsors the plan.

- An education savings plan lets individuals open an investment account for a beneficiary's future education expenses. Funds in an education savings plan can be used for qualified education expenses like tuition, fees, and room and board. Education savings plans are more versatile than prepaid tuition plans because investment funds can be used at any college or university. Qualified expenses include tuition up to $10,000 per student per year at an elementary or secondary public, private, or religious school. This includes two-year and four-year institutions, vocational and trade schools, and postgraduate programs. It doesn't matter in which state the beneficiary's school is located.

When you make contributions to a 529 account, they are not deductible for federal income tax purposes; however, your state may offer tax benefits such as a reduction in state income tax. And lifetime contribution limits are quite generous—up to $300,000 or more depending on the state.

The main advantage of a typical 529 plan is tax-free earnings. If you withdraw funds from a 529 plan for qualified education expenses for the designated beneficiary, your earnings aren't subject to federal income tax nor, in some cases, state income tax. However, if these funds aren't used for qualified education expenses, your earnings on nonqualified withdrawals will be subject to federal income tax and an additional 10 percent federal tax penalty. You may also be subject to state and local income taxes.

These 529 plans are a great way to invest funds for your children's college expenses. These investments can grow tax free if you use them for qualified higher education expenses or tuition for elementary or secondary schools. If you would like to find out more information about a 529 plan, the National Association of State Treasurers created the College Savings Plan Network at http://www.collegesavings.org/, where you can find links to most 529 plan websites.

Of course, the obvious question on every parent's mind is, "How much should I save for my child's college education?" A college education can be a worthwhile, but expensive, experience. In fact, education costs have been increasing year after year and outpace inflation. In the past decade, tuition and fees at an in-state public institution increased 3.2 percent more than inflation, while private college costs increased 2.4 percent more than inflation.[51] As a result, the average cost for tuition and room and board at an in-state public institution is almost $21,000 per year, while it's almost $47,000 at a private institution.[52]

Many students will not pay the full "sticker price" because of financial aid and scholarships, but college will be a significant investment for most students. After grants and scholarships, students will still pay about $15,000 per year at an in-state public school and almost $27,000 at a private college.[53] Just like retirement funds, any amount you can save and invest on a regular basis will help, and the earlier you start investing in a 529 plan, the greater potential for growth and tax benefits. However, like all investments, these plans do have some risk, so be sure to read the plan's offering circular carefully to understand the fine print, pertinent restrictions, and eligible expenses.

Protecting Your Future through Life Insurance

Like an emergency fund, another way to prepare for future needs is through life insurance. Traditionally, life insurance is a way to protect your family from a loss of income if a primary wage earner passes away unexpectedly. It is one method to transfer this risk from your family to your insurance provider. Life insurance proceeds can help take care of burial expenses, provide living expenses for a surviving spouse and children in the home, or pay off a mortgage or other debt. If your budget can afford it, life insurance is a great tool to take care of your loved ones and ensure your financial goals are met if the unexpected happens.

The question of how much life insurance you need depends on your unique situation. Are you single or married? Are you the sole wage earner in your family? Do you have young children living at home? Do you have substantial debt or a mortgage? The answers to these questions can help you determine if you need life insurance and how much. As you pay down debt, as your children grow up and leave home, and as you fully fund your emergency fund, there's less need for a life insurance policy and the monthly expense associated with the premiums.

As an illustration, let's say you're a newlywed who just purchased a three-bedroom home with plans to start a family. A thirty-year term life insurance policy for $250,000 can help your family replace your earnings, pay off your mortgage, or cover your children's college education if you pass away within the next thirty years. For as low as $18 per month for a male, or $14 per month for a female, this is a relatively small expense to help bring you peace of mind and take care of your family.[54] When the insurance term is up in thirty years, it may not be necessary to renew your policy if your mortgage is paid off, your children are living on their own, and you have a well-funded emergency fund and a healthy retirement account.

The main benefit of life insurance is the tax-free, lump-sum death benefit paid to the beneficiary. But some life insurance policies have other benefits to consider. For example, while traditional term life insurance policies provide a payment when the insured person dies, whole life policies combine the benefits of a term policy with a savings account. As you make payments on your policy, part of the payment is used to build the policy's cash value. This cash value grows over time and the insured can borrow against it. In other words, a whole life policy provides the benefit of a term policy with the added benefit of "requiring" the insured to make contributions into a savings account. These premiums are higher than a term life insurance policy but do provide a benefit that might be useful in your specific situation. A life insurance agent or financial planner can help you decide which type of insurance policy will provide the greatest benefits in your specific situation.

Tips for Success

Once you decide to start an emergency fund, a three- to six-month goal may seem overwhelming. In this case, consider the lesson from the children's fable about the tortoise and the hare: slow and steady wins the race. In fact, that's the lesson from Proverbs 13:11. God promises that "whoever gathers little by little will increase it" (ESV). Even saving little by little, God promises you'll have increase.

Your financial journey isn't a sprint; it's a marathon. Concentrating on the end goal may seem daunting. Instead, focus on the small steps that will lead you to your goal of building an emergency fund. Start by saving $500, and then increase your savings to $1,000. From there, increase your emergency fund to an amount equal to one month of expenses. After that, strive for three months or more.

Here are a few more tips to help you increase your savings:

- Redirect all bonuses, cash gifts, or salary increases to your emergency fund.

- After you pay down your debt, reallocate those monthly funds used for credit card or loan payments to increase your savings.
- Use automatic withdrawal or direct deposit to make monthly transfers to an account created just for an emergency fund.
- Separate your emergency fund from other savings accounts. Open a second savings account for other specific purposes, such as Christmas gifts, vacation, or a new automobile.
- Once you reach a specific savings goal, reward yourself. It can make the journey more fun.

If one of your financial goals is to save money for your child's college education, consider a 529 plan. Investments in a 529 savings plan can have greater benefits and growth than letting your funds sit in a regular savings account or certificate of deposit. You can invest funds in a 529 plan in the same type of securities as retirement funds, which have the potential for significant growth. And if these funds are used for qualified education expenses, you don't have to pay tax on your investment earnings.

If you start investing when your child is young, even saving a little bit each month can be significant. For example, if you start saving $50 per month when your child is born, you'll have invested $10,800 by the time your child turns eighteen. If your investments can earn 6 percent per year, which is a conservative estimate based on historical growth in the stock market, your college fund can grow to over $19,000, which can help pay for your child's first year of college. If you can increase your contributions or increase your rate of return, your growth will be even greater.

Marty and Jennifer's Story

Marty and I remember sitting in a church service two years ago praying about what our missions pledge should be. We weren't in a healthy financial situation to make a gift or a pledge that fit within our budget, but we knew God would be at work in whatever amount we pledged.

We had credit card debt that we really wanted to pay off, but we didn't have the resources to pay it off. It was $8,000. Finances were tight and we went a little further behind each month, but we felt God say that we should put Him first and He would take care of the rest. We were already tithing at 15 percent, giving God our firstfruits. Now He was asking us to put Him ahead of our desires, our debt, and other commitments. So, we did! We fasted for twenty-one days—twice—and at the top of our prayer list was fulfilling our missions promise, paying off our credit card debt, and increasing our income to meet our family needs.

A few months later, Marty's employer offered him a new position that would require our family to move, but also included a substantial pay raise. After fasting and praying a lot with our friends, we laid out a "fleece," and his employer met the criteria for us to accept the offer. We sold our home in Missouri, which we had only bought two years before, and bought a home in the new city. In buying a new home, we had enough from the sale to meet the down payment requirement on the new home (after realtor fees, etc.) and had $8,000 left over, which is a miracle because the housing market was higher in our new location. However, God worked it out!

We had no idea when we made our missions pledge that we would be moving, or that we could make a profit selling our home that would enable us to fulfill our pledge. Had we not made a missions pledge and instead tried to pay off the credit card debt, we would have missed out on God's continual blessing. (As a side note, the home we sold in Missouri had sat vacant for two years before we bought it. God saved it for us and for that missions pledge to increase our faith and fulfill His work.)

To follow up on that blessing, Marty's company got new management six months into the move. They let everyone go, even though they had just paid to move us six months earlier. We knew that God had something better in mind for us, and we weren't worried—the best was yet to come because God is our planner.

We had applied for foster care a year before, and our license was approved. We got three foster children the week before Marty lost his job. Thankfully, he got a severance package. It was as if he was being paid to stay home with our new family and children who had never had a good father. Later, another company sought him out and offered almost double what he had been paid before. With the increase in salary, we were able to pay off the credit card debt.

Our foster children have made personal commitments to Christ, and we are likely to have an adoption finalized next year. We couldn't have imagined any of this: moving, selling our house, fulfilling the missions promise, losing one job and getting another at double the salary, or adopting three children. We are so thankful for God's abundance in our lives and thankful that we put Him first in our finances.

Prayer

Heavenly Father, help me take comfort in Your promise that saving little by little will result in financial increase. Help me to not get overwhelmed with my savings goal but to remain diligent and committed to the journey. Amen.

Action Steps

1. Start a short-term emergency fund by saving $500 and working up to $1,000. What immediate steps can you take to create margin for this goal?

2. Determine what your long-term emergency fund should be to cover your essential expenses for three months or more.

3. Create a plan to increase your emergency fund to three months or more. What long-term steps can you take to create margin for this goal?

4. If you're married, discuss the savings goals you have as a couple. Besides a short-term and long-term emergency fund, what other savings goals do you have?

What steps can you take to achieve these goals?

Step 9
Invest in Yourself

"For I know the plans I have for you, declares the Lord, *plans for welfare and not for evil, to give you a future and a hope." Jeremiah 29:11, ESV*

Many adults have difficulty planning for their financial needs during retirement. This includes 28 percent of adults who don't have adequate savings for retirement, and up to 50 percent who won't be able to maintain their current standard of living during retirement.[55, 56] Even when people have started saving for retirement, 53 percent don't feel comfortable making investment decisions about their retirement accounts.[57] In this step, we will discuss a few strategies for making your wealth last through retirement.

Types of Retirement Funding

For most adults, there are three main components to retirement funding: Social Security, personal investments and savings, and employer-provided pensions. Most adults will need a combination of these funding streams to live comfortably, although many companies have moved away from offering pensions. Let's briefly look at each of these funding types.

Social Security

The Social Security program was created in 1935 to provide income to retired workers age sixty-five and older. The Social Security Administration uses thirty-five years of your highest eligible earnings to calculate your retirement benefits. If eligible, you can apply for Social Security benefits as early as age sixty-two or as late as age seventy. Your monthly retirement benefit is based on your full retirement age, which is somewhere between sixty-five and sixty-seven depending on your date of birth. If you apply before your full retirement age, your monthly benefit will be reduced. If you apply after your full retirement age, your monthly benefit will increase. The longer you delay applying, the more you'll receive in your monthly benefit. One in six Americans currently receives benefits from Social Security.

Since Social Security was created in the 1930s, the average lifespan of retirees has increased and there are more retirees receiving assistance. For example, the average lifespan for females has increased by five years, and there were five times more retirees in 2000 than in 1930.[58]

There's a lot of speculation about the stability and longevity of the Social Security program. I suspect our government officials will do everything in their power to make sure the program remains in some form for many years to come. However, you shouldn't count on Social Security benefits to take care of all your needs during retirement. Social Security is only meant as a supplement to other retirement savings. Currently, Social Security benefits only replace about 40 percent of the average income before retirement.[59]

With that in mind, be sure to maximize your Social Security retirement benefits when the time comes to retire. A conversation with a financial planner or retirement consultant will help you decide when to sign up for benefits based on your unique circumstances. The Social Security Administration has useful articles and resources on their website. You can review your estimated Social Security benefits, use their online calculators, and even sign up for benefits at https://www.ssa.gov.

Individual Retirement Account and Personal Savings

Since Social Security will only replace 40 percent of your preretirement income, most adults will need personal savings and investments to maintain their current standard of living during retirement.

In step 8 we discussed the importance of personal savings for emergencies. For most adults, this emergency fund will be kept in a low-interest savings account or invested in a short-term instrument like a certificate of deposit (CD). However, to maximize your earning potential, you should also consider investment options where your funds can earn a higher rate of interest between now and retirement. Investing is simply a long-term strategy to build wealth. With the combination of long-term investments and tax-deferred or tax-free accounts, an investor can build wealth for retirement.

Two popular options for retirement savings are individual retirement accounts, or IRAs, and employer-sponsored plans, like a 401(k). In 2017, the average balance of a 401(k) was almost $100,000 and the average balance for an IRA was slightly higher at $103,500.[60] For adults age sixty-five to sixty-nine and on the verge of retirement, the average IRA balance in 2013 was almost $213,000.[61]

Individual Retirement Accounts: Two types of IRAs are traditional and Roth. Contributions to a traditional IRA are tax-deductible, but the retiree will pay income tax on the distributions during retirement. Contributions to a Roth IRA are not tax-deductible, but the retiree will not pay income tax on the distributions during retirement. Both types are popular, but you may want to talk with a financial planner to determine if one may be more beneficial than the other for your needs.

Employer-Sponsored Plans: An employer-sponsored plan is generally called a 401(k) plan, based on the section number in the IRS code where it is authorized. Much like a 401(k) plan, some public schools, churches, and 501(c)(3) charities offer a 403(b) plan.

These plans are also known as defined contribution plans and 47 percent of private employers offer these plans.[62] Whether a 401(k) or 403(b) plan, these employer-sponsored plans allow employees to make contributions through payroll deductions. Many employers also offer automatic contributions or matching contributions. This means the employer will help fund the employee's retirement account! This increases the impact of the employee's contribution.

For self-employed people, there are other retirement plans called SEP, Simple IRA, and Solo-401(k).[63] Similar to the other retirement plans, there are specific contribution limits and tax implications. Again, a discussion with a financial planner can help you decide which investment tool is best for you.

Pension

A pension, often called a defined benefit plan, is a retirement plan maintained by an employer to provide fixed payments to employees when they retire. The retirement payments are based on the employee's salary and total years of employment.

The success and growth of an employer pension fund is driven by a combination of market returns and annual employer contributions. If market returns are low, the employer may need to make additional contributions to ensure enough funds exist to pay all pensions. As a result, the longevity and stability of pension funds may be dependent on the longevity and stability of the employer.

While popular in the past, many employers have been phasing out pension plans over the past thirty years. In fact, only 8 percent of private companies offer a defined benefit plan to employees.[64]

How Much Do I Need?

Whether you have an individual retirement account, an employer-sponsored plan, or a combination of both, these investment options make saving for retirement relatively simple, but there are other important factors to consider. Life expectancy is increasing, so you need to plan on having a retirement nest egg that will last you between eighteen and twenty-five years.

There are three main questions that impact your retirement goals: (1) What do you want to do during retirement? (2) When do you want to retire? and (3) How much do you need to save for retirement?

The question of how much to save doesn't have a one-size-fits-all answer. While financial experts recommend saving at least 9 to 17 percent of your income each year for retirement, everyone's needs will be different during retirement. Therefore, everyone's total retirement nest egg and investment strategy will be different. However, a few principles apply to most everyone.

Financial experts estimate that during retirement you should plan on needing between 70 to 90 percent of your current income if you want to maintain your current standard of living. This amount will depend on whether your house is paid off, children are still living at home, and your overall health. However, some retirees may increase their expenses during retirement if they take up a new hobby or travel more.

Another concern during retirement is health care. A retired couple during retirement can expect to pay up to $275,000 on insurance premiums, copayments, deductibles, and prescription drug expenses.[65] This is after the amount that Medicare or private insurance will pay! For this reason, many workers will have to wait until age sixty-five or later to retire to ensure they have adequate health care. If you want to retire before age sixty-five, you should plan on obtaining private insurance to cover your health needs until you can sign up for Medicare.

With health care costs for a retired couple at $275,000 and retirees living up to twenty-five years during retirement, it's important to be prepared financially for your retirement. It's wise to start preparing early. On average, people start to prepare for retirement around age forty-five, but most adults should start saving for retirement much, much earlier.

Here's a general guideline to know if you are saving enough for retirement:[66]

- By age 30, save the equivalent of your annual salary.
- By age 40, save three times your annual salary.
- By age 50, save six times your annual salary.
- By age 60, save eight times your annual salary.
- By age 67, save ten times your annual salary.

Think about this: Assuming you spend 4 percent of your nest egg each year during retirement, a total portfolio of $1 million dollars invested in 60 percent stocks and 40 percent bonds would last at least thirty years for adults retiring in 1980. However, due to market returns and inflation, that same portfolio is expected to last only twenty-five years for adults retiring in 2013.[67] It's impossible to predict how the market will perform in the future, but this demonstrates the importance of diligent and thoughtful planning for retirement.

Retirement experts are sounding the alarm that many, if not a majority of, families won't be able to maintain their standard of living during retirement. One measurement tool is called the National Retirement Risk Index. It estimates that over 50 percent of working-age families are at risk of being unable to maintain their standard of living during retirement. This is up from 31 percent in the 1980s.[68]

The Power of Compound Interest

The most important step you can take in your retirement planning is to start early. Retirement savings, whether in an employer-sponsored 401(k) or a personal IRA, will generally be invested in marketable securities that earn interest. The type of securities will depend on your risk tolerance, which determines the interest rate of return.

The longer you let your money earn interest, the greater it can grow. The value of compound interest is the fact that your money saved for retirement will earn interest, and then your interest will earn interest.

Consider the following scenarios to demonstrate the potential earning power of letting your money grow over time.

Scenario 1: My daughter Taylor, at age twenty, starts investing $4,000 a year in a retirement account that earns 8 percent interest each year. She contributes for five years and at age twenty-five she stops all contributions. By her twenty-fifth birthday, she will have invested $20,000 in her retirement account. With the power of compound interest over forty-five years, her $20,000 investment will be valued at over $594,500 at age sixty-five.

Scenario 2: My son Aaron waits until age forty-five to start investing for retirement. He invests $10,000 per year for the next twenty years and at age sixty-five he will have invested $200,000. If he also earns 8 percent interest each year, his retirement account will grow to just under $491,000.

Even though Aaron invested ten times more than Taylor, she will end up with $100,000 more in her investment account due to the power of compound interest over a longer time.

Let me illustrate it another way. I call this illustration "the cost of waiting." If you wait too long to start saving for retirement, it will be hard to catch up. Let's say Taylor starts saving $3,000 per year, at 8 percent interest starting at age twenty-five. Her brother Aaron also starts saving $3,000 per year, at 8 percent interest, but doesn't start until age thirty.

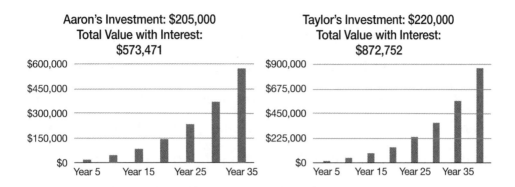

In forty years, Taylor will only have invested $15,000 more than her brother Aaron, but with the power of compound interest, she will have a total retirement savings of almost $873,000, which is substantially larger (almost $300,000 more) than her brother's retirement savings. By waiting even a few years to start saving, Aaron will be at a significant disadvantage. As a result, it may mean Aaron will have to work longer and delay retirement in order to have enough savings to support all his needs during his golden years of retirement.

Unfortunately, this may be a common predicament for many young adults because most people delay saving for retirement until they have a higher wage and more disposable income. As a result, the average age to start saving for retirement is forty-five. However, these illustrations demonstrate that the earlier you start saving for retirement the better, because you'll be using compound interest to your advantage.

Tips for Success

The most common reason people don't save for retirement is because they believe they don't make enough money. The second most common reason is because they struggle to pay all their bills.[69] If you have similar reasons, it's vitally important to change your behavior and your budget. Go back to the budget you created in step 6 and review it to see if you can find more margin to put toward retirement. Let these illustrations motivate you to make saving for retirement one of your highest goals.

If you're like most adults and starting to save late in life or don't have much margin to devote to retirement, don't feel overwhelmed. Start investing whatever amount you can. Find an amount or percentage you can allocate for retirement contributions now. Then seek to increase this amount by 1 percent every year. If you get an annual wage increase, allocate that increase directly to your retirement fund.

If your employer sponsors a retirement plan, take advantage of it. In fact, you should maximize your earning potential by making the maximum contributions available in your plan and getting the employer to match, when available. After you max out your employer-sponsored plan, it will probably also be necessary for you to start an individual retirement account.

Finally, seek help from a qualified financial planner to discuss strategies specific to your financial situation and retirement goals.

John and Mary's Story

I (Mary) was raised in a church denomination that rarely spoke of tithing, but the offering basket was passed every Sunday, and I would put a few dollars in it. One Sunday, I remember a pastor gave a sermon on tithing, so I filled out a pledge form and started tithing. Ten years later I committed my life to the Lord and started a brand-new journey.

I have a passion for missions. When the missionaries came to church my heart was so touched! But while my husband, John, went on many missions trips, I stayed home with my kids. Instead, God gave me the gift of giving, and it has grown in my spirit. Sometimes I sense a still small voice urging me to give, sometimes I dream about a missionary, and sometimes when I'm driving I think of a missionary. I believe these are all God's ways of directing my giving.

I retired from nursing two years ago and thought I wouldn't be able to give as much, but not so. God has supplied all our needs! In fact, after hearing about a missions project in Mexico, I told John, "I want to do that." Six months later, John and I went on a missions trip to Ensenada, Mexico. I never imagined I would go to Mexico to help build houses, but God did!

One day I said to the Lord, "I don't know how we're going to pay for this Lord, but if you supply the need, we'll keep going." God has met our needs all these years. Even in retirement, we can bless others financially. I will keep giving and going because there's a whole world that needs to know the love of God.

Prayer

Heavenly Father, I know You have a plan for my future. Help me to participate in this plan by finding margin to invest in my future. Help me to stay committed to this long-term plan. Amen.

Action Steps

1. If available to you, make sure you fully understand the benefits of your employer-provided pension or defined benefit plan. For example, if you remain at that company until you retire, what is your expected retirement benefit?

2. Take advantage of any employer-sponsored 401(k), 403(b), or defined contribution plan available to you. If your employer offers matching contributions, take advantage of the maximum contribution possible. What steps can you take to find additional margin to maximize your contributions?

3. Whether you have other retirement options or not, consider opening a traditional or Roth IRA. Maximize your earning potential by saving early and letting compound interest work to your advantage. Keep reviewing your budget to identify margin that can be devoted to retirement contributions.

4. Consider meeting with a qualified financial planner to discuss strategies for your specific retirement goals.

5. Make a list of the types of activities and lifestyle you hope to have during retirement. If you're married, what are your dreams for retirement as a couple?

Do you estimate that this lifestyle will cost less, the same as, or more than your current lifestyle?

Do you think your current retirement funding goals are adequate to cover your planned activities?

If not, what changes do you need to make so your retirement dreams can become a reality?

Step 10
Bless Others

"A good man leaves an inheritance to his children's children, but the sinner's wealth is laid up for the righteous."
Proverbs 13:22, ESV

Though this is the last step in our journey, you may find the message of this step provides the motivation to work through all the other steps. Once you've taken control of your finances, you're able to be generous and bless others. Whether you desire to give to charities and religious programs, children's programs, hunger and poverty programs, educational programs or environmental programs, by creating margin in your finances, reducing debt, and investing in your future, you'll gain the freedom to bless others financially.

A common theme that runs throughout Scripture is the topic of generosity. You can't read far without observing God's generosity to mankind, Christ's generosity to the lost, and a Christ-follower's generosity to others. Here are just a few examples where Scripture calls us to be generous toward others:

It is well with the man who deals generously and lends; who conducts his affairs with justice.
(Psalm 112:5, ESV)

Honor the LORD with your wealth and with the firstfruits of all your produce; then your barns will be filled with plenty, and your vats will be bursting with wine. (Proverbs 3:9–10, ESV)

One gives freely, yet grows all the richer; another withholds what he should give, and only suffers want. Whoever brings blessing will be enriched, and one who waters will himself be watered. (Proverbs 11:24–25, ESV)

Whoever is generous to the poor lends to the LORD, and he will repay him for his deed.
(Proverbs 19:17, ESV)

Whoever has a bountiful eye will be blessed, for he shares his bread with the poor. (Proverbs 22:9, ESV)

Whoever gives to the poor will not want, but he who hides his eyes will get many a curse.
(Proverbs 28:27, ESV)

The point is this: whoever sows sparingly will also reap sparingly, and whoever sows bountifully will also reap bountifully. (2 Corinthians 9:6, ESV)

As for the rich in this present age, charge them not to be haughty, nor to set their hopes on the uncertainty of riches, but on God, who richly provides us with everything to enjoy. They are to do good, to be rich in good works, to be generous and ready to share, thus storing up treasure for themselves as a good foundation for the future, so that they may take hold of that which is truly life. (1 Timothy 6:17–19, ESV)

Do not neglect to do good and to share what you have, for such sacrifices are pleasing to God. (Hebrews 13:16, ESV)

Did you notice how these Scriptures all point to the blessing God promises when we're generous with others, including with our finances? God even promises that the generous person won't lack anything or be in want but will be blessed; God will be pleased, and the giver will be richly rewarded. What an amazing promise! And rest assured that God keeps His promises!

Let me encourage you not to wait until step 10 to be generous. Remember what I mentioned in step 1? Even though you might be tempted or advised to stop all charitable giving while you're getting control of your finances, that's backward thinking. Seek God's direction as you complete each step. As you respond to His leading and are generous with others, God will be generous with you.

Can Money Buy Happiness?

Would it surprise you to know that science can back up these scriptural principles? You've probably heard, or even repeated, the saying, "Money can't buy happiness." What if I told you that science has proved that oft-repeated phrase wrong! Consider the following studies:[70]

- In one study, researchers gave participants either $5 or $20 and asked the participants to spend the money on themselves or others. When assessing the participant's happiness, those who spent the money on others were happier than those who spent the money on themselves. Interestingly, the amount of money was not a factor.

- Another study surveyed employees who received a profit-sharing bonus. The research found that the amount of the bonus spent on others predicted the employee's happiness up to eight weeks later. They couldn't make the same prediction for employees who spent the bonus on themselves.

- In a third study, researchers found a positive relationship between the amount of money given to charity or spent on others and the person's general happiness.

Whether stated in Scripture or proved by science, I know these principles have been true in my life, and I fully expect you'll experience the blessing that comes by being generous with others, if you haven't already.

Leave a Legacy

The writer of Proverbs says a good man leaves an inheritance—not only to his children, but to his grandchildren (Proverbs 13:22). What a wonderful legacy: leaving an inheritance that impacts the next two generations!

So, what does an inheritance consist of? Leaving an inheritance for your children and grandchildren can certainly include a financial component, but it can be much more than that. We can create a lasting impact on the next two generations by passing on our values, family traditions, and most importantly, a spiritual heritage. Yes, we can bless our children financially through wills, trusts, and other estate planning tools, but it's also important to leave a legacy by training our children how to manage and take control of their own finances.

In fact, only 56 percent of retirees expect to leave an inheritance to their children.[71] Most others don't think they'll have anything left over to pass on. But remember, leaving an inheritance isn't just leaving what you earned, but also what you learned.[72]

My prayer for you is that you'll have assets to leave to your heirs as a result of following the steps in this book; but more important than financial assets, I want you to pass on life-changing principles and behaviors.

I don't want my children, or your children, to end up like many of the statistics highlighted throughout this book. Let's use the principles in this book to train the next generation so our children and grandchildren will use budgets to manage their spending; will avoid unnecessary debt and actively get out from under debt as soon as possible; will use credit cards responsibly; will set financial goals for their future and track their progress on a regular basis, including short-term and long-term savings goals; will proactively invest in their own future through retirement planning; and will continue this cultural shift by leaving a similar legacy for their children and grandchildren.

Tips for Success

Here are some ways you can bless others and leave a legacy for your children and grandchildren:

- Be generous to others! Share your time, talents, and resources with those in need. Volunteer at a local food pantry, soup kitchen, or other charity to be a blessing to others.

- Model good behavior for others. Let your life be an example to those who follow you. While money can be a private topic, people in your life can learn from your struggles and successes. For example, children whose parents were good savers tend to become good savers themselves.

- Help your children understand the principles of contentment and moderation. Whether it relates to name-brand clothing, the latest gadget, or the newest gaming system, teach your children to be content in all things and wise with their money.

- Help your children earn money so you can teach them to save, give, and spend wisely while they're still living at home.

- Teach your children the principles of budgeting, creating margin, and setting goals for their financial futures. Have them write down the name and price of a special toy, electronic gadget, or clothing item that they want, and help them earn and save money to buy it themselves.

- Open a bank account with your children and teach them the principles of compound interest by reviewing the investing scenarios in step 9.

Maybe you grew up in a household where no one provided this type of training, so you made some unwise choices with your money and struggled financially. Unfortunately, your children may fall into the same trap. Without proper training, this cycle may be repeated for many generations. The good news is you can make a positive impact not only for your children but for future generations by modeling these concepts and teaching these principles to your children.

Rollie and Tammy's Story

Tammy and I have always been tithers. In fact, as a kid, I started tithing on the income from my paper route. It was relatively easy to believe that 10 percent of my income was God's. It was the remaining 90 percent that was open to negotiation. When we married, I soon realized that Tammy was also big on giving to special ministry projects, benevolence needs, and missionary endeavors. Anytime someone presented a special ministry opportunity, Tammy was ready to give. I was willing to give, too, if I had some extra money to give up.

But after a few years, God started to change my attitudes about giving. Instead of making the final decision on how much we would give to missions my responsibility, Tammy and I started praying together for what God wanted us to give. Amazingly, God always gave each of us the same number. It was exciting to know that we were hearing from God. It was also exciting to me to know that the amounts He requested were still within our budget.

Just as soon as we learned how to listen to what God wanted us to give, He started to double what He was asking! I remember He asked us to double our commitment to missions for four years straight! It was still exciting to do it, but it was getting close to being more than we could afford.

A short time later, our church started a building campaign and asked members to make a three-year commitment to the project. "Impacting Generations through Extravagant Giving" was the theme. As soon as we heard about the building campaign, we started to pray about the commitment God wanted us to make. Immediately, Tammy and I both settled in on $25,000 over three years. It took us a few days to get used to the idea of committing to such a large sum, but we were willing to do it. However, we soon became uneasy about this number—not because it was a lot of money, but because Tammy and I both were hearing God tell us to double our commitment to $50,000. Looking back, we can see that He'd been laying the groundwork for this request over the past five years.

There were two priorities in our lives at that time: using extra funds to pay off our mortgage—our last remaining debt—in the next five years and moving into our dream house on a cul-de-sac with a two-car garage, workshop, swimming pool, and big yard. But with this huge commitment, we had to put our priorities on hold. Even with money in our savings, and reducing expenses at home, we still didn't have enough income to meet this large commitment.

Believe it or not, that didn't scare us—it excited us! Tammy and I knew without a shadow of a doubt that we had heard from God and we obeyed. We did what we knew to do—we postponed our dreams and cut expenses at home. We still didn't know how God would help us meet our commitment, but we were sure that He would, because it was His request.

As we agreed on our commitment, we also agreed that all our resources were at His disposal, so we asked God what He wanted to do through us. We agreed that everything we had was "on the table" and available for God. Over the next two years God took us on an unbelievable journey of faith, and through that journey revealed His faithfulness to us over and over.

For example, as soon as we made our commitment, I knew God was asking us to give a stock investment to the campaign within the next few months as a firstfruits offering. The stock investment was only $16,000, so I would rather have waited until the end of the campaign to let the stock grow. However, it was clear to us that we needed to transfer the stock as soon as possible, so we started the process.

What God knew was that our stock investment would double to $32,000 by the time the transfer was completed and liquidated by the church. What God also knew was that this same stock was getting ready for a downturn. If I had waited until the end of the building campaign to transfer the stock, it would only have been worth $6,900. Tammy and I would never have been able to complete our commitment of $50,000 without trusting and obeying God from the beginning of this adventure.

Soon after, we knew God was telling us to pay off our commitment a year before the campaign ended. It took a lot of sacrifice to make the additional payments to complete our pledge, but with God's help, we did that—exactly two years after we made our firstfruits offering. Once again, God revealed why. That same day, I was contacted to interview for a job in another state. God was moving us from this church to another, and He opened the door to allow me to merge my talents as an auditor with full-time ministry. God used this stewardship journey to deepen and mature our relationship with Him. We've learned to trust Him in every aspect of our lives and can believe Him when He says He will provide for us in the future.

Prayer

Father God, help me to be generous with my money and to bless others. Help me to leave a legacy of blessing for my children and grandchildren by teaching and modeling these principles. May You be glorified through my actions. Amen.

Action Steps

1. Review the Scriptures highlighted in this step. Did any specific passage resonate with you? Why?

2. What are some ways you can be generous to others with your finances?

3. If you have children, what steps can you take to train them to manage and control their own finances successfully?

4. If you're married, what are some ways as a couple you can show generosity to others and share these principles with your friends and family?

Epilogue

*"Let us not become weary in doing good,
for at the proper time we will reap a harvest
if we do not give up." Galatians 6:9*

Congratulations! You've completed these ten steps and are on your way to a life of financial freedom. Whether it took you a few days or a few months, you created a plan to reduce your reliance on credit cards and debt, you established financial goals for your future, you created a spending plan to take control of your money, and you identified ways to create enough margin in your budget to achieve those goals. I want you to know that the principles you've learned in this book will help you achieve a life with less debt and financial stress, increased confidence in your current and future financial situation, and harmony in your home and relationships.

I must be honest with you: Reaching the end of this book doesn't mean you've successfully reached the end of your financial journey. Rather, it's just beginning!

Continuing the Journey

The step-by-step process I describe in this book is designed to help you see how the principles and tasks in each step build upon each other. The result is an accessible model that can help you gain control of your finances. But this model isn't meant to be used once and then discarded. To gain the long-term financial success you desire, you'll want to review these principles and worksheets on a regular basis and evaluate whether you need to make a course correction.

Here's why. As we continue down the road called life, changes occur. In fact, all living things undergo change. We change jobs, we marry, we have kids, we move, we get sick, we start new hobbies, and we set new goals. Every time we experience change in our lives, we must evaluate our current financial situation and see if we need to adjust our spending plan. For example:

- As you progress in your profession or move from job to job, hopefully your income will increase. When you have additional income to add to your spending plan, you'll need to determine where you'll allocate this extra margin. Will you pay off debt or save it for your emergency fund or add it to your retirement fund?
- If you decide to start a family, this will certainly create new expenses for your family. How will you change your

spending plan to absorb these new expenses? Do you still have the same margin at the end of the month to meet your current savings goals, or will you need to make adjustments?

- If you're unexpectedly injured or fall ill for a long period of time, you may not only lose income because you aren't able to work, but you may have increased medical expenses. This will require a significant change to your current spending plan since it affects income and expenses. Will you have enough income each month to cover all your bills? Do you have an emergency fund to help cover your lost income? Will you have to delay other savings goals to cover current expenses?

If there's one guarantee in life, it's that life will change. That's why it's wise to evaluate your financial situation on a regular basis to make sure you're still headed in the right direction to achieve your financial goals.

Next Steps

Now that you've finished the book, make a commitment to review your financial progress at least annually. Here are some things to consider during your annual review:

1. Review your progress on reducing debt. Have you been able to pay off any debts? Have you identified additional funds to apply to your debt to maintain your momentum? Have you incurred new debt that you need to add to the debt snowball worksheet?

2. Update the Net Worth Worksheet you created in step 4 and review your progress. Does it agree with the financial goals you created in the same step?

3. Evaluate your spending plan. Take note of any changes in your income or spending habits that might not be reflected on your spending plan and create an updated spending plan. Do you still have margin at the end of the month?

4. Review steps 6 and 7 to benchmark your activity and see if there are additional ways to increase margin in your budget.

5. Evaluate your emergency fund. Have you replenished your short-term emergency fund if you had to use it during the year? Are you still saving money to achieve a long-term emergency fund equal to at least three months of expenses?

6. Review your retirement goals created in step 9 and evaluate your progress. If available, have you signed up for your employer-provided retirement program or taken

advantage of matching retirement contributions? If not, what changes can you make to your spending plan to allow this?

7. Evaluate how you are blessing others on your own financial journey. Review the Scriptures highlighted in step 10. Are you generous to others as Scripture calls you to be? Are you leaving a legacy to the next generation by sharing the financial principles you learned in this book?

If you experience any significant life-change such as a different job, a promotion, a change in your marital status, or having a child, go ahead and evaluate your spending plan at that time. Don't wait for an entire year to pass before you take stock of your current situation.

I've added additional worksheets at the end of this book that you can use to update your debt snowball progress, evaluate your net worth, create new financial goals, track financial activity, or create a new spending plan. Additionally, digital versions of all the worksheets contained in this book are available to download and print at BalancedBudgetBalancedLife.com/worksheets.

While the model I describe in this book is sequential, you don't have to complete each step before moving on to the next. It's acceptable (and oftentimes necessary) to be working on several steps at the same time. For example, you don't have to completely pay off all debt identified in step 3 before you start saving for retirement in step 9. Similarly, you don't have to complete the first 9 steps before you endeavor to be generous in step 10. Scripture is clear that it's important to your financial health that you are consistently generous with others.

I also think it's equally important to save money for your short-term emergency fund early in your journey. In fact, having an emergency fund may be one of the first steps to conquer since having a financial cushion will help you feel financially secure and will reduce stress. If an unexpected expense occurs, it won't completely derail your financial progress because you'll be prepared to absorb it.

I stated in the introduction that my prayer for you is that this book will motivate you to create a financial plan and change the trajectory of your life. I know God wants this for you as well. Seek God's help as you complete each step and never forget He has a heavenly storehouse to meet your every need.

Appendix A
102 Ways to Earn More, Spend Less and Create More Margin

Ways to Increase Income

- Sell things on Facebook, Craigslist, eBay; use an online selling service.
- Have a yard sale.
- Take items to a resale shop.
- Transition to a smaller, more economical car and house.
- Sell the kids' outgrown clothing, toys, and collectibles.
- Get a second job (deliver pizza, cashier, wait person).
- Start a home-based business (childcare, walk dogs , mow lawns).
- Involve your kids; help them see it's the family household budget.
- Get a roommate or rent out a spare bedroom.

Ways to Spend Less

Groceries

- Compile a shopping list and stick to it.
- Plan menus for the week and include meals for leftovers.
- Buy generic or store brands.
- Look at expiration dates on food before you buy.
- Buy in bulk when reasonable.
- Use coupons; go on double-coupon day.
- Avoid prepared, pre-cut, and packaged meals.
- Don't shop when you're hungry.
- Shop when you're in a hurry.
- Leave the kids at home.
- Avoid vending machines.
- Use a reusable water bottle instead of buying bottled water.
- Make your own baby food.

Eating Out

- Eat out fewer times.
- Cook at home—make it a family project and involve the entire family.
- Use discount coupon books.
- Visit half-price websites like Groupon.
- Take advantage of "kids eat free" nights.
- Share meals.

- Purchase from the appetizer list.
- Order from lunch or early-bird menus.
- Order water, not soft drinks.
- Take home any leftovers.
- Watch for coupons on restaurant websites.
- Sign up for restaurants' email specials and free meals on birthdays.
- Make your coffee at home and skip the coffee shop.
- Take your lunch to work.

Entertainment

- Use discount coupon books.
- Visit half-price websites like Groupon.
- Rent movies at home instead of going to the theater. Alternatives: Netflix, Redbox, Hulu, Amazon Prime.
- Check any memberships (AAA, AARP, Sam's Club, credit card) for discount offers.
- Go to the library or read online instead of purchasing subscriptions.
- Entertain at home. Consider potlucks to share costs.
- Play board games or outdoor games as a family.
- Go to nature parks, bike paths in your own neighborhood; make exercise a family event.
- Check your local library for free events and activities for kids.

- Pack a lunch instead of purchasing food at ballparks or amusement parks.
- Visit local zoos and museums, especially on free days or special discount days.

Gifts and Holidays

- Save for Christmas and birthday gifts all year; stick to a limit.
- Reduce the number of people you buy for or buy one gift for the entire family.
- Plan and shop online for discounts.
- Increase the number of potluck parties you host instead of dinner parties.
- Give time instead of gifts; volunteer or serve as a family.
- Take a family vacation instead of buying gifts.
- Make homemade gifts.
- Use artificial Christmas tree instead of real.

Clothing

- Buy on sale and off-season.
- Shop at secondhand or thrift stores.
- Buy dual-purpose clothing; consider basic colors for greater combinations.
- Shop for name-brand clothes at discount stores and outlets.
- Sign up for loyalty reward programs.

- Mend clothes instead of replacing.
- Avoid impulse buying.
- Avoid clothes that are dry-clean only, or use home dry-cleaning kits.
- Avoid trendy or fad fashions.
- Swap clothes with a friend.

Banking and Credit Cards

- Balance your checkbook.
- Pay your bills on time to avoid late fees.
- Get overdraft protection on checking accounts.
- Pay cash and avoid financing deals—including "no interest for 90 days."
- Pay off credit cards; use the debt snowball method.
- Make payments automatically and on time with online banking.
- Choose credit cards without annual fees.
- Select a cash-back or rewards credit card.
- Look for a credit card with lower interest rates.
- Avoid ATM fees.
- Increase credit score for better rates on loans.

Insurance and Automobile

- Include insurance costs when comparing cars to purchase.
- Shop around for insurance; ask for multipolicy discounts (home and auto).

- Raise your deductibles to reduce premiums.

- Increase your credit score for better insurance rates.

- Drive smarter; maintain a clean driving record.

- Avoid behaviors that raise insurance rates: smoking, riding motorcycles, getting speeding tickets.

- Purchase used cars and keep them longer.

- Get regular tune-ups and maintain proper tire pressure, fluid levels, and other maintenance.

- Ride with coworkers.

- Consolidate your errands with friends.

- Walk or bike when possible.

Utilities

- Give up the home phone if you have a cell phone.

- Reduce or eliminate Internet, cable, pay-per-view, multiple streaming services.

- Get out of cell phone contract; consider prepaid plans.

- Question line items on phone bills, credit cards, cable, and cell phone bills.

- Unplug electrical items to conserve energy.

- Use low-watt light bulbs.

- Lower your thermostat in winter and raise it in summer.

- Lower your water heater temperature setting.

Other Ideas

- Refinance your house—seek help from a trusted expert to see if it's worthwhile.
- Change your withholding to reduce your annual tax refund and increase monthly margin.
- Reuse plastic shopping bags for garbage or carrying your lunch.
- Visit the library instead of buying books; if you buy books, buy used.
- Compare prices before buying any major purchase.
- Wait thirty days before any major purchase.
- Plan for vacations and set a budget.

Note: This list is a compilation of ideas from the author and the following sites:

- http://www.dumblittleman.com/2008/01/30-easy-ways-to-save-money-and-no-you.html (accessed March 20, 2019)
- https://www.forbes.com/sites/laurashin/2016/08/30/101-ways-to-save-money/ (accessed March 20, 2019)
- http://www.101waystosavemoney.com/ (accessed 2011; site no longer available)

Debt Snowball Worksheet

List your debts from smallest to largest.

This is the amount of extra money you can use to pay down debt.

Debt / Creditor *Example*	Total Payoff	Interest Rate	Minimum Payment	New Payment (Minimum Payment + Extra Cash)
Credit Card	$1,800	19.5%	$55	$55 + $100 = $155
Car Loan	$5,000	5.5%	$250	
School Loan	$25,000	7.5%	$300	

Debt / Creditor	Total Payoff	Interest Rate	Minimum Payment	New Payment (Minimum Payment + Extra Cash)
~~Credit Card~~	~~$1,800~~	~~19.5%~~	~~$55~~	~~$155~~
Car Loan	$5,000	5.5%	$250	$250 + $155 = $405
School Loan	$25,000	7.5%	$300	

After the first debt is paid off, use the extra funds to pay off the next debt.

Debt / Creditor	Total Payoff	Interest Rate	Minimum Payment	New Payment (Minimum Payment + Extra Cash)

Debt Ratio Worksheet

Debt to Income Ratio

Total Monthly Debt Payments $ _____

Total Monthly Gross Income   ÷ $ _____

        ×   100

       _____ percent

Housing Expense Ratio

Total Monthly Housing Payments $ _____

Total Monthly Gross Income   ÷ $ _____

        ×   100

       _____ percent

Debt to Income Ratio (goal is less than 35–40 percent)

To compute this ratio, calculate your total monthly debt payments. Include mortgage or rent payments, credit card minimum payments, auto loan payments, and any other loan payments. Divide your total monthly debt payments by your total monthly gross income. Multiply this result by 100 to get a percentage.

Housing Expense Ratio (goal is less than 28 percent)

To compute this ratio, calculate total monthly housing expenses. Include mortgage or rent payments, interest, real estate taxes, homeowner insurance, and association fees. Divide your total monthly housing expenses by your total monthly gross income. Multiply this result by 100 to get a percentage.

Net Worth Worksheet

Assets			Market Value
	Cash		
		Cash on Hand	
		Checking and Savings	
		Certificates of Deposit (CD)	
		Cash Value of Life Insurance	
	Investment and Retirement		
		Stocks and Bonds	
		Mutual Funds	
		Pension	
		IRA / 401K / 403B	
		529 College Savings	
	Property		
		Principle Residence	
		Second Residence	
		Home Furnishings	
		Automobiles	
		Collectibles	
		Jewelry	
	Other		
Total Assets			

Liabilities			Amount Owed
	Unsecured Debt		
		Credit Cards	
		Charge Accounts	
		Student Loans	
		Alimony / Child Support	

Liabilities cont'd			Amount Owed
		Unpaid Taxes	
		Other	
	Secured Debt		
		Home Mortgage	
		Home Equity Loans	
		Auto Loans	
		Boats / RVs / Campers	
		Other	
Total Liabilities			
Net Worth (Assets Minus Liabilities)			

Financial Goals Worksheet

Goal (include the "Why?")	Strategy or Action Steps	When Do I Start?	When Do I End?

Weekly Income and Expense Worksheet

	Category								
Week Number ___									
Sunday									
Monday									
Tuesday									
Wednesday									
Thursday									
Friday									
Saturday									
Subtotals									

Total Income _____

less Total Expenses _____

Net Surplus / Deficit _____

Weekly Income and Expense Worksheet

	Category								
Week Number ____									
Sunday									
Monday									
Tuesday									
Wednesday									
Thursday									
Friday									
Saturday									
Subtotals									

Total Income _____

less Total Expenses _____

Net Surplus / Deficit _____

Monthly Income and Expense Worksheet

	Category								
Day									
1									
2									
3									
4									
5									
6									
7									
8									
9									
10									
11									
12									
13									
14									
15									
16									
17									
18									
19									
20									
Sub-total									

	Category									
Day										
21										
22										
23										
24										
25										
26										
27										
28										
29										
30										
31										
Total										

Total Income _____

less Total Expenses _____

Net Surplus / Deficit _____

Monthly Spending Plan Worksheet

	Monthly Totals
Income	
Gross income (paychecks, other income)	$
Less taxes (federal, state, Social Security, and Medicare)	$
Net Monthly Income	$
Expenses	$
Charity — Tithes, offerings, charitable gifts	$
Housing — Mortgage or rent	$
Homeowners and rental insurance	$
Utilities (electric, water, gas, trash)	$
Phone, Internet, cable	$
Real estate taxes	$
Maintenance and repairs	$
Other housing expenses	$
Food — Groceries	$
Dining out	$
Other food expenses	$
Transportation — Gas, parking, and public transportation	$
Car maintenance	$
Car insurance, license, and taxes	$
Car loan payment	$
Other transportation expenses	$
Health — Medicine and prescriptions	$
Medical and dental insurance	$
Life insurance	$
Other health expenses	$

		Monthly Totals
Personal and Family	Clothing	$
	Toiletries and cosmetics	$
	Childcare, school supplies	$
	Child support	$
	Gifts	$
	Entertainment	$
	Pets	$
	Hobbies	$
	Other personal and family expenses	$
Other	Credit card payment	$
	Student loan payment	$
	Miscellaneous	$
Savings	Emergency fund	$
	Retirement	$
	College fund	$
	Extra payments to pay down debt	$
	Other savings goals	$
	Total Monthly Expenses	$

Total Income _____

less Total Expenses _____

Net Surplus / Deficit _____

Spending Plan Definitions

Income	Gross income (salary, wages, side jobs, dividends, interest, other income)
Charity	Tithes, offerings, charitable gifts
Housing	Mortgage or rent payments, homeowner or rental insurance, utilities (electric, water, gas, trash, phone, Internet, cable or satellite television), real estate taxes, maintenance and repairs, and other housing expenses
Food	Groceries, dining out, and other food expenses
Transportation	Auto loan or lease payments, gasoline, oil, and maintenance, public transportation, parking, tolls, auto insurance, registration, taxes, and other transportation expenses
Health	Medicine and prescriptions, insurance premiums for medical, dental and life, and other health expenses
Personal & Family	Clothing, toiletries, cosmetics, childcare, child support, school supplies and activities, gift, entertainment, pets, hobbies, and other personal and family expenses
Other	Credit card minimum payments, student loan payments, and other monthly debt payments
Savings	Emergency fund, retirement contributions, college savings fund, extra payments to pay down debt, and other savings goals

NOTES

1. Kelley Holland, "We Know Why You and Your Spouse Will Fight Tonight," CNBC, February 4, 2015, http://www.cnbc.com/2015/02/04/money-is-the-leading-cause-of-stress-in-relationships.html (accessed January 24, 2018).

2. Gerri Detweiler, "Love and Money: What Statistics Say," *Business Insider*, February 14, 2012, http://www.businessinsider.com/love-and-money-what-statistics-say-2012-2 (accessed January 24, 2018).

3. "Financial Statistics," *Money Habitudes*, June 20, 2017, http://www.moneyhabitudes.com/financial-statistics/ (accessed January 24, 2018).

4. Detweiler, "Love and Money."

5. Jason Heath, "Why Money Issues Still Ruin Marriages," *Financial Post*, July 16, 2013, http://business.financialpost.com/personal-finance/why-money-issues-still-ruin-marriages (accessed January 24, 2018).

6. Dennis Jacobe, "One in Three Americans Prepare a Detailed Household Budget" Gallup.com, June 3, 2013, http://news.gallup.com/poll/162872/one-three-americans-prepare-detailed-household-budget.aspx (accessed July 2, 2018).

7. Quentin Fottrell, "Half of American Families Are Living Paycheck to Paycheck," *MarketWatch*, April 30, 2017, http://www.marketwatch.com/story/half-of-americans-are-desperately-living-paycheck-to-paycheck-2017-04-04 (accessed July 2, 2018).

8. Fottrell, "Paycheck to Paycheck."

9. "Two-Thirds of Minimum Wage Workers Can't Make Ends Meet, CareerBuilder Survey Finds," *CareerBuilder*, August 11, 2016, http://www.careerbuilder.com/share/aboutus/pressreleasesdetail.aspx?ed=12%2F31%2F2016 (accessed July 2, 2018).

10. Fottrell, "Paycheck to Paycheck."

11. *CareerBuilder*, "Can't Make Ends Meet."

12. Arielle Vogel, "What Does the Bible Say About Credit Cards?" Crown, July 10, 2017, http://www.crown.org/blog/what-does-the-bible-say-about-credit-cards/ (accessed January 27, 2018).

13. Rakesh Kochhar, "How Americans Compare with the Global Middle Class," Pew Research Center, July 9, 2015, http://www.pewresearch.org/fact-tank/2015/07/09/how-americans-compare-with-the-global-middle-class/ (accessed March 3, 2018).

14. Randall K. Barton, *Discovering Financial Success, Leader's Guide* (Springfield, MO: Gospel Publishing House, 2001), 9.

15. Barton, *Discovering Financial Success*, 12.

16. Gary G. Hoag, *Faith and Finances: A Stewardship Curriculum for Schools and Churches* (Franklin, TN: Seedbed Publishing, 2017), 30.

17. Barton, *Discovering Financial Success*, 20.

18. "An Ameriprise Study on Couples and Money," Ameriprise Financial, September 2016, https://www.ameriprise.com/cm/groups/public/@amp/@ameriprise/documents/document/p-014230.pdf, 3–4 (accessed March 22, 2019).

19. *Money Habitudes*, "Financial Statistics."

20. "U.S. Personal Saving Rate, 1970-2012," The Hamilton Project, March 14, 2013, http://www.hamiltonproject.org/charts/u.s._personal_saving_rate_1970-2012 (accessed February 11, 2018).

21. Rebecca Lake, "23 Dizzying Average American Savings Statistics," CreditDonkey, last modified May 18, 2016, http://www.creditdonkey.com/average-american-savings-statistics.html (accessed February 10, 2018).

22. Lake, "23 Dizzying Average American Savings Statistics."

23. "Credit Card Rate Report," CreditCards.com, April 4, 2018, https://www.creditcards.com/credit-card-news.php (accessed April 14, 2018).

24. Larry Burkett, *The Complete Guide to Managing Your Money* (New York: Inspirational Press, 1996), 41.

25. Dilip Soman, "Effects of Payment Mechanism on Spending Behavior: The Role of Rehearsal and Immediacy of Payments," *Journal of Consumer Research* (February 2001): 460–74.

26. Barbara Bennett, Douglas Conover, Shaun O'Brien, and Ross Advincula, "Cash Continues to Play a Key Role in Consumer Spending: Evidence from the Diary of Consumer Payment Choice," Federal Reserve Bank of San Francisco, April 29, 2014, https://www.frbsf.org/cash/publications/fed-notes/2014/april/cash-consumer-spending-payment-diary/ (accessed April 14, 2018).

27. Adapted from David Weliver, "Why (Most) People Stay in Debt," chart, *Money Under 30*, September 1, 2017, https://web.archive.org/web/20190424155250/https://www.moneyunder30.com/get-out-of-debt-on-your-own (accessed May 17, 2019).

28. Benjamin Franklin, *Poor Richard's Almanack*, quoted in Simran Khurana, "Famous Quotes about Money," *ThoughtCo.*, March 7, 2019, https://www.thoughtco.com/quotes-about-money-2831124 (accessed March 22, 2019).

29. Erin El Issa, "2017 American Household Credit Card Debt Study," NerdWallet, June 2018, https://www.nerdwallet.com/blog/average-credit-card-debt-household/ (accessed November 13, 2018).

30. *Money Habitudes*, "Financial Statistics."

31. Some people might suggest starting with the debt with the highest interest rate, as opposed to the lowest balance (called the Debt Avalanche method). Social studies have shown that the success achieved by paying off the smallest debt first actually helps motivate people to remain committed to the long-term process. See Robert Berger, "Debt Snowball Versus Debt Avalanche: What the Academic Research Shows," *Forbes*, July 20, 2017, https://www.forbes.com/sites/robertberger/2017/07/20/debt-snowball-versus-debt-avalanche-what-the-academic-research-shows/#7d6078d91454 (accessed April 17, 2018).

32. El Issa, "2017 American Household Credit Card Debt Study."

33. "SMART Goals: How to Make Your Goals Achievable," MindTools, http://www.mindtools.com/pages/article/smart-goals.htm (accessed February 11, 2018).

34. Anne Tergesen, "Forget the 4% Rule: Rethinking Common Retirement Beliefs," *The Wall Street Journal*, February 9, 2018, https://www.wsj.com/articles/forget-the-4-rule-rethinking-common-retirement-beliefs-1518172201

(accessed February 11, 2018).

35. For more information on what documents you should keep, visit this website: http://articles.extension.org/pages/11023/ organize-your-important-household-papers:-print-this-lesson.

36. Detweiler, "Love and Money."

37. Adapted from Kregg Hood, *From Debt to Life: 10 Proven Steps to Beat Credit & Build Financial Freedom* (self-published, 2004), 48–49.

38. "Consumer Expenditures in 2016," U.S. Bureau of Labor Statistics, April 2018, https://www.bls.gov/opub/reports/consumer-expenditures/2016/ pdf/home.pdf (accessed July 14, 2018).

39. The 50/30/20 guideline is recommended by U.S. Senator Elizabeth Warren and her daughter Amelia Warren Tyagi in their book, *All Your Worth*. Several financial experts and websites also advocate this plan. For more information, see Elizabeth Warren and Amelia Warren Tyagi, *All Your Worth: The Ultimate Lifetime Money Plan* (New York: Free Press, 2005).

40. "Millennials Are Spending More Money on Coffee Than Retirement Plans," *Fox News*, January 18, 2017, http://www.foxnews.com/food-drink/2017/01/18/millennials-are-spending-more-money-on-coffee-than-retirement-plans.html (accessed July 2, 2018).

41. "Visa: Americans Report They Spend an Average of $2,746 on Lunch Yearly," VISA, November 4, 2015, https://investor.visa.com/news/news-details/2015/Visa-Americans-Report-They-Spend-an-Average-of-2746-on-Lunch-Yearly/default.aspx (accessed July 2, 2018).

42. James Clear, "How Long Does It Actually Take to Form a New Habit? (Backed by Science)," https://jamesclear.com/new-habit (accessed April 16, 2018).

43. A simple Internet search will identify several personal finance programs and applications that may be helpful.

44. Fottrell, "Paycheck to Paycheck."

45. Daniel Corrin, "New Data on U.S. Savings Rate," Savings and Retirement Foundation, August 13, 2013, http://savingsandretirement. org/2013/08/13/new-data-on-u-s-savings-rate/ (accessed July 14, 2018). See

also U.S. Bureau of Economic Analysis, "Personal Saving Rate [PSAVERT]" chart, retrieved from FRED, Federal Reserve Bank of St. Louis; https://fred. stlouisfed.org/series/PSAVERT (accessed July 13, 2018).

46. Franklin, "The Way to Wealth."

47. "Financial Well Being in America," Consumer Financial Protection Bureau, September 26, 2017, https://www.consumerfinance.gov/data-research/research-reports/financial-well-being-america/ (accessed July 2, 2018), 53.

48. Fottrell, "Paycheck to Paycheck."

49. *CareerBuilder*, "Can't Make Ends Meet."

50. As of August 2018. For more information about specific plans, visit the College Savings Plan Network at http://www.collegesavings.org/.

51. "Average Rates of Growth of Published Charges by Decade," The College Board, https://trends.collegeboard.org/college-pricing/figures-tables/ average-rates-growth-published-charges-decade (accessed August 18, 2018).

52. "Average Published Undergraduate Charges by Sector and by Carnegie Classification, 2017-18," The College Board, "https://trends.collegeboard.org/college-pricing/figures-tables/average-published-undergraduate-charges-sector-2017-18 (accessed August 18, 2018).

53. "Average Net Price over Time for Full-Time Students, by Sector," The College Board, https://trends.collegeboard.org/college-pricing/figures-tables/average-net-price-over-time-full-time-students-sector (accessed August 18, 2018).

54. Quotes obtained August 19, 2018 from Geico Insurance, https://www.geico.com.

55. "Federal Reserve Board Issues Report on the Economic Well-Being of U.S. Households," Federal Reserve, last updated May 19, 2017, https://www.federalreserve.gov/newsevents/pressreleases/other20170519a.htm (accessed July 2, 2018).

56. Chris Kahn, "Retirement Statistics: Then vs. Now" (slideshow), Bankrate, July 17, 2013, https://www.bankrate.com/retirement/retirement-statistics-then-vs-now/#slide=5, accessed March 25, 2018. See also "National

Retirement Risk Index," Center for Retirement Research at Boston College, http://crr.bc.edu/special-projects/national-retirement-risk-index/ (accessed April 16, 2018).

57. Federal Reserve, "Economic Well-Being of U.S. Households."

58. "Life Expectancy for Social Security," Social Security Administration, https://www.ssa.gov/history/lifeexpect.html (accessed March 30, 2018).

59. "Suze Orman on Why Creating an Account is Important," video, Social Security Administration, https://www.ssa.gov/myaccount/ (accessed March 30, 2018).

60. Donna Fuscaldo, "Fidelity: Average 401k and IRA Balances Up 10% in 2017," *Investopedia*, November 6, 2017, https://www.investopedia.com/news/fidelity-average-401k-and-ira-balances-10-2017/ (accessed March 30, 2018).

61. Sean Williams, "Here's How Much the Average American Has in an IRA, Sorted by Age," *The Motley Fool*, June 27, 2016, https://www.fool.com/retirement/2016/06/27/heres-how-much-the-average-american-has-in-an-ira.aspx (accessed March 30, 2018).

62. "Establishments Offering Retirement and Healthcare Benefits: Private Industry Workers," table, Bureau of Labor Statistics, March 2017, https://www.bls.gov/ncs/ebs/benefits/2017/ownership/private/table01a.pdf (accessed March 31, 2018).

63. "Retirement Plans for Self-Employed People," Internal Revenue Service, last updated April 24, 2018, https://www.irs.gov/retirement-plans/retirement-plans-for-self-employed-people (accessed July 8, 2018).

64. Bureau of Labor Statistics, "Establishments Offering Retirement and Healthcare Benefits."

65. "Health Care Costs for Retirees Rise to an Estimated $275,000 Fidelity Analysis Shows," *Fidelity*, August, 24, 2017, https://www.fidelity.com/about-fidelity/employer-services/health-care-costs-for-retirees-rise (accessed July 14, 2018).

66. Fidelity Viewpoints, "How Much Do I Need to Save For Retirement?"

Fidelity, June 5, 2017, https://www.fidelity.com/viewpoints/retirement/how-much-money-do-i-need-to-retire (accessed July 14, 2018.

67. Chris Kahn, "Retirement Statistics: Then vs. Now," slideshow, Bankrate, July 17, 2013, https://www.bankrate.com/retirement/retirement-statistics-then-vs-now/#slide=1, accessed March 25, 2018.

68. Alicia H. Munnell, Wenliang Hou, and Geoffrey T. Sanzenbacher, "National Retirement Risk Index Shows Modest Improvement," Center for Retirement Research at Boston College, January 2018, Number 18–1, http://crr.bc.edu/wp-content/uploads/2017/12/IB_18-1.pdf (accessed July 14, 2018). See also Chris Kahn, "Retirement Statistics: Then vs. Now," slideshow, Bankrate, July 17, 2013, https://www.bankrate.com/retirement/retirement-statistics-then-vs-now/#slide=5 (accessed March 25, 2018).

69. Cameron Huddleston, "Survey Find 42% of Americans Will Retire Broke—Here's Why," Go Banking Rates, March 6, 2018, https://www.gobankingrates.com/retirement/planning/why-americans-will-retire-broke/ (accessed April 15, 2018).

70. Christopher Peterson, "Money and Happiness," *Psychology Today*, June 6, 2008, https://www.psychologytoday.com/blog/the-good-life/200806/money-and-happiness (accessed July 8, 2018).

71. Chris Hogan, "What Financial Legacy Are You Leaving Behind?" *ChrisHogan360*, https://www.chrishogan360.com/what-financial-legacy-are-you-leaving-behind/ (accessed November 17, 2018).

72. Bruna Martinuzzi, "What Type of Legacy Do You Want to Leave?" AmericanExpress, November 24, 2014, https://www.americanexpress.com/en-us/business/trends-and-insights/articles/want-legacy/ (accessed November 17, 2018).

ACKNOWLEDGMENTS

I'm grateful to my friends Matt and Stephanie, Marty and Jennifer, Josh and Laura, Thomas and Noelle, Donavon and Erin, Mark and Katie, Christian and Emilie, Troy and Angela, Gary and Jan, and John and Mary. Thank you for sharing your stories with me. I know your stories will inspire others to trust God with their finances while practicing the principles in this book.

ABOUT THE AUTHOR

Rollie Dimos is a husband, father, writer, speaker, teacher, traveler, and pizza enthusiast. The director of internal audit at the Assemblies of God national office, he also oversees the AG Center for Leadership and Stewardship Excellence. In these roles, he reviews financial reports, evaluates financial processes, and discusses financial principles with pastors and leaders in the church. His passion is to help church leaders reduce the risk of fraud and increase financial accountability and integrity.

Professional recognitions include the certified fraud examiner, certified internal auditor, and certified information systems auditor certificates. Previously, Rollie was an audit supervisor with the U.S. Army Audit Agency, where he was recognized for his professional accomplishments with the Commander's Award for Civilian Service and the Achievement Medal for Civilian Service. With auditing experience in the government and nonprofit sectors, Rollie has been helping leaders assess the strength of their financial and organizational controls for over thirty years.

He is the author of *Integrity at Stake: Safeguarding Your Church from Financial Fraud* (Zondervan, 2016) and an earlier, self-published version titled *Integrity at Stake: Safeguarding*

Your Church's Honor (2014). His self-published book was awarded second place in the finance category of the 2014 Christian Author Awards hosted by Xulon Press.

A frequent writer and speaker for church leaders, pastors, and ministry students on the topics of corporate finance, personal finance, and church administration, he oversees and writes articles for *Church Administration Essentials*, a monthly newsletter that provides targeted resources for church pastors, board members, and bookkeepers. He has also published an article in *Influence* magazine.

A graduate of Evangel University and the Assemblies of God Theological Seminary, Rollie currently resides in Ozark, Missouri, with his wife and children.

FOR MORE INFORMATION

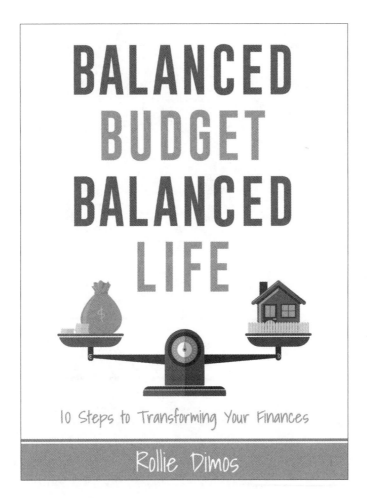

For more information about this
book and other helpful resources,
visit **www.MyHealthyChurch.com**.